Becoming the Best in Our Field

The Team Unit Leader's Workbook

Introducing the *Triangle Team Leadership Model*: *Becoming the Best in Our Field*, a process that will help team unit leaders transform themselves and their direct reports into champion performers and the team unit into a championship/profitable organization

By Michael V. Mulligan Ph.D. C.M.F
Executive Business and Career Coach
(847) 981-5725

i

THE TRIANGLE TEAM LEADERSHIP MODEL

Becoming the Best in Our Field

The Team Unit Leader's Workbook

---

iUniverse books may be ordered through booksellers or by contacting:

iUniverse LLC
1663 Liberty Drive
Bloomington, IN 47403
www.iuniverse.com
1-800-Authors (1-800-288-4677)

ISBN: 978-1-4502-5958-3 (sc)
ISBN: 978-1-4502-5959-0 (e)

Printed in the United States of America
iUniverse rev. date: 05/02/2014

A Meaningful Quote

"Success comes to those

who become success conscious.

Failure comes to those

Who indifferently allow themselves

to become failure conscious"

Napoleon Hill

Comments from the Author

This workbook describes the *Triangle Team Leadership Model: Becoming the Best in Our Field* process. It was written to help executives, managers, supervisors and coaches develop a plan, that if met, would make them one of the best team unit leaders in their functional area and industry. If you ask why a department, division and an organization is successful, it is the team unit leader working with and through his/her direct reports to achieve their business plan that makes it happen. If you ask why individuals reach their potential, are happy at work, perform at high levels, advance in their career and remain with their company, it has to do with how well team unit leaders lead, manage, mentor and bring out the best in their direct reports.

I have personally worked with over 2,500 individuals who were dismissed from their company and when I asked them to list the number one reason for the separation, over 90% said it had to do with the working relationship between them and their boss. A boss or team unit leader can bring out the best in their direct reports or kill their spirit driving them out the door. It has been said over and over if the team players between two competitors are fairly equal, it is the coaching that will make the difference.

I had the honor of playing on six championship teams in high school and college. The major reason those six teams became champions was because we had outstanding coaches. Our coaches ran the right system with the type of players we had on the team and placed individuals in the positions that matched their talent and strengths. They worked our players until they became the best at their positions and consequently they won many honors. Our coaches told us to believe in ourselves, not to back away from challenges and never give up until the game was over. The challenge of "being the best at my position" was planted in my mind and has never left me.

The goal of this workbook is to help you, the team unit leader, develop a plan that will transform you, your team unit and direct reports into the best in your work fields. We have created a *Seven Step Process* to help you achieve this goal. We will ask you to complete a number of tasks in each *Step* to complete the *Seven Step Process*.

Step One – I will define leadership, review how other professionals define leadership and discuss why it is so important to have effective unit leaders today.

Step Two- You will *review the importance of business planning* -We will discuss why it is important to create a business plan and how the *Gap Analysis and Closure Model* and *Task Empowerment Process* can help you in developing and meeting the objectives in your plan.

Step Three- You will review the *Triangle Team Leadership Model: Becoming the Best in Our Field.* You will learn the thinking behind the *Model,* the phases of the *Model*, the motivator selected to inspire employees and the *Team Engagement Achievement Motivation* Program that is used to launch and execute the *Model.*

Step Four- You will *focus first on the bottom or support side of the triangle- The Team Unit Leader's Plan-* You need to assess yourself and establish and meet personal growth objectives. As you develop your leadership and management skills, you will be more effective in helping your direct reports establish and meet their champion building objectives. Once the objectives are met, you and your direct reports can be labeled as champion performers and the unit a championship/profitable team.

Step Five - Next, you will *focus on the left side of the triangle- The Team Unit Plan.* You will conduct research on your competition and ask your direct reports, customers and other stakeholders to evaluate your organization and unit. You will review the vision and mission statement of your company or organization and the past performance of your organization and unit (division or department). Then you will review the organization's champion building goals and objectives for next year and write objectives for your unit that tie into the organization's objectives.

Step Six- *You will focus lastly on the right side of the triangle-The Team Members' Plans.* You as the team unit leader should meet with each direct report One-On-One and review the vision and mission statements and "best in our field" objectives for the corporation and your unit (division, department or group). You want your direct reports to endorse the objectives plus suggest additional "best in our field" objectives. You will also put your direct reports through assessment and add personal growth" objectives to their list. You need to identify the objectives and tasks that direct reports needs to complete to meet these specific objectives The *Task Empowerment Process* explained in *Step Three* can be used to help each direct report become an expert in executing all the tasks assigned to him or her

Step Seven- You need to establish your *Performance Evaluation Team* and finalize your champion building objectives for yourself, your unit and then direct reports. You also need to develop a method to monitor and measure everyone's progress and success.

In conclusion, if you are a team unit leader who wants to transform your direct reports, unit and yourself into the best to advance careers and help the organization be successful, you need to execute a process like the *Triangle Team Leadership Model: Becoming the Best in Our Field.* If all employees can establish champion building objectives that are aligned to the development of themselves, their unit, division and company and achieve them, all in the organization will be rewarded financially, personally and professionally.

Michael V. Mulligan Ph.D. CMF
Executive Business/Career Coach

Table of Contents

Dreams never hurt anybody

if you keeps working behind the dream

to make as much of it come real as you can.

Frank W. Woolworth

Step One

Review the Different Views on Leadership

We would like you to complete the following *three tasks* to complete *Step One.*

Page

Task One- Review Dr. Mulligan's Thoughts on Leadership

While most professionals throw out the word leadership in a general way, Dr. Mulligan says people play two leadership roles – **The Team Unit Leader** and **The Team Member Leader**. Employees will be asked to be a team unit leader leading and managing a group of people and at other times they will be asked to be a team member leader operating as a player on the team specializing in doing certain tasks to help the team unit leader and unit meet their predetermined objectives. Each leadership role requires an individual to perform special tasks. Employees need to understand and perform the tasks that are required to play both leadership roles. Listed below is an example of how unit leadership and member leadership can be broken down in a large organization.

The Team Unit Leaders	Team Member Leaders
Chairman of the Board	**Board Members**
C Suite Officers	
Chief Executive Officer/President	**Chief Level Officers**
Chief Level Officers	**Senior Vice Presidents**
(Chief Administrator)	
(Chief Economist)	
(Chief Engineer)	
(Chief Financial Officer)	
(Chief Human Resource Officer)	
(Chief Legal Officer)	
(Chief Marketing Officer)	
(Chief Operating Officer)	
(Chief Sales Officer)	
(Chief Technology Officer)	
Senior Vice Presidents	**Vice Presidents**
Vice Presidents	**Directors**
Directors	**Managers**
Managers	**Supervisors**
Supervisors	**Project Managers**
Project Managers	**Regular Workers**

If a company has a number of divisions as well as a corporate office, there will be more opportunity to move up the management ladder. In a smaller organization, you will not have as many steps on the management ladder so you have a better chance to reach the C Suite and move into a Chief Level position sooner if that is your goal.

Unit Leaders can be appointed to their positions, elected or be part of a search. Many large companies have set up leadership pipelines or succession planning strategies to keep talented unit leaders moving through the pipeline to the top. If a company doesn't have a leadership pipeline in place, they will probably pay a lot of money to retained search firms to recruit talent. One should keep in mind that you can move to Chairman/CEO quickly if you can start your own business and make it be successful.

Team Unit leaders who occupy the C Suite or in senior level positions are held more accountable for the bottom line or making profit. They must determine the products or services the organization will offer, who the customers will be, who will make the products or deliver them, who will sell the products or services and who will collect the money and pay the bills and keep the sales and profit numbers up to date. They have to plan organize, hire and manage the people who will help them be successful.

Team Unit leaders who occupy the C Suite or in high level senior positions want to surround themselves with self managers or people who are self directed and experts at doing their tasks so they can focus on planning, setting "best in our field" objectives and developing and executing strategies that will help the organization be successful. They don't see themselves spending much time as a coach and counselor to their direct reports.

Vice Presidents and below will be responsible for more One-On-One counseling and coaching and keeping the communication flowing from the Senior Management team to all employees in the organization. Vice Presidents, directors, managers and supervisors are like the coaches on a football team. They are in charge of certain aspects of the business and they must turn their direct reports into expert performers in their functional area (accounting, finance, human resources, legal, logistics, marketing, sales, technology, etc.) and the unit into the best so the total organization runs smoothly and succeeds.

The team unit leaders at the vice president level and below must figure out away to excite and unite everyone on the "best in our field" objectives set by senior management. This leader strives to be an expert in working with and through people to set and achieve growth objectives that will motivate and benefit all. The team unit leader is given authority to hire and fire those reporting to him or her.

The Team Member Leader is responsible for managing only himself. He/she has no one reporting to him or her and doesn't have the authority to hire or fire people. This individual must be a team player and be a follower helping the team unit leader and team unit be successful. This person strives to be an expert in a functional area implementing specific tasks that help the team unit achieve it's objectives. Such a position could be an accountant, engineer, human resource specialist, logistics expert, programmer, , sales person, researcher, underwriter, security person etc. They later are recognized in their organization as an expert leader in a special area or performing certain tasks. Unit leaders do become a team member when they walk in the office of their boss.

Unit leaders need to select the work environment where they can be more effective.- For example, some individuals want to and are capable of leading an entire organization while others prefer to lead a small group of people. Also, there are individuals who would be a better unit leader in a highly structured bureaucratic environment where change is slow. There are others who would thrive in a highly competitive environment where change occurs often. Also, there are those who should run their own business than work and report to someone else.

3

People in both leadership roles want to be empowered (given position power) if they are held accountable for specific results.

If team unit or team member leaders are held accountable to set and meet "best in our field' objectives, they want to be empowered (given <u>position power</u> -) or given the authority to complete tasks the way they were trained or their way. One might be given a lot of responsibility, but without position power or authority, it is difficult to accept ownership for meeting or failing to meet objectives. It is only fair if you are going to make someone accountable for the results, you should give them the authority to do the job.

Dr. Mulligan recommends using the *Task Empowerment Process* with direct reports. The unit leaders sits down with his/her direct report and identifies the tasks one has to execute to meet a specific objective. Once the direct report becomes an expert in executing the tasks, he/she is empowered or given full authority to execute the task on his/her own. Of course, the task needs to be labeled in terms of importance to the company. If you are closing a big sale with a major client, maybe the boss wants to be present with the sales person even if the sales person is one of your best.

Team unit leaders might feel more comfortable moving from being a micro-manger (close supervision) to a macro-manger (no supervision) when working with direct reports on important tasks. This way you can coach the direct report and know when they are an expert in carrying out the task.

Leadership by example is a good phrase but you need to identify what values and behavior you want people to emulate

Unit leaders should have their direct reports take the *Personal Values Assessment Survey,* the *Performance Facilitator Assessment Survey* and the *Helper Communicator Assessment Survey* and identify the values and behavior you want people on the team to emulate. Then people can lead by example reinforcing the values and behavior set by the team.

All unit leaders must be an effective One-on-One Idiosyncratic Manager

One-On-One *Idiosyncratic Management* is knowing the personality, capabilities and what motivates each of your direct reports. Some people can handle pressure situations and others can't. Some people need to be complimented more often than others. The more you know the strengths and weaknesses of your direct reports, you can then put them in the right positions and help them succeed. One-On-One Idiosyncratic Management is extremely important in the development of individuals, teams and organizations.

Team unit leaders need to become an expert on assessment surveys to learn about individuals that report to them and become efficient in meeting One-On- One with direct reports to develop the tasks that need to be completed to meet the predetermined objectives. You can only manage individuals not groups of people. One-On-One meetings can help a unit leader control the behavior of individuals in team meetings.

.

Dr. Mulligan's Three Stage One-On-One Performance Facilitation/Helping Process

1. *Stage One*- The manager should build a working relationship with his/her direct reports. He/she should develop some commonality, learn to respond with empathy, shows respect to the individual by believing the individual has the capability to come up with a plan and solve his/her own problems. A mutual and reciprocal trust is essential. The manager takes the time to build a rapport with his/her people so they feel comfortable in sharing.

2. *Stage Two*- The manager has developed an engaging relationship where sharing of ideas are done without fear of being ridiculed or criticized. The direct report and the manager agree on the objectives that need to be met and identify the tasks that need to be completed to meet each objective. This participative/democratic style relationship allows employees to have input in the decision making and planning process. As the manager learns what tasks the direct report can execute alone, he empowers or gives them authority to execute them. This approach advocates a team-oriented environment where everyone is expected to contribute to the plan and success of the organization. The action starts to pick up.

3. *Stage Three*- The manager has put his direct reports into the execution stage. He/she continues to meet with them monitoring their progress making changes where necessary to meet the predetermined objectives. The team members are now moving at a very high speed playing as a team unit. The manager can now become confrontational when team members aren't performing because they know he/she cares about them.

Unit leaders must develop their personal power to obtain more position power and gain followers
A team unit and team member leader should also learn how to develop their personal power. This is learning how to build rapport with others and operate as a performance facilitator and helping communicator. Leaders need to work on their personal power first so people like them, respect them and want to follow them. Dr. Mulligan wrote *Sharpening My One-On-One Performance Facilitation and Helping Communication Skills* to help individuals learn how to develop personal power and help others make important decisions and solve their own problems and issues

Functions of a Manager
Dr. Mulligan says team unit leaders also need excellent management skills in the areas of planning, organizing, directing, coordinating and controlling to be successful.
Management is defined as setting pre-determined objectives with your direct reports and working with and through them to meet the objectives.
Planning and Budgeting-What are we aiming for & what monies do we take in and spend?
Organizing- Who is involved and how?
Directing-Who is doing what and when?
Coordinating-Who informs who and about what?
Controlling- Who judges the results and by what standards

Situational Leadership and Management

Many unit leader's management style could be branded by others depending on their actions. We will discuss three leadership/ management styles.

- ❖ **The Autocratic/Dictator Approach**

- ❖ **The Democratic Approach**

- ❖ **The Consensus Approach**

The **Autocratic/Dictator Approach** is where one person decides what the plan is going to be. He/she gains input and information from others but makes the decision himself or herself. He/she believes the buck stops with the boss.

The **Democratic Approach** is where the unit leader discusses a situation or problem with a number of people and the majority vote (51%) decides what the solution or plan should be. Decisions can be made by more than half the people.

The **Consensus Approach** is where the unit leader discusses a situation or problem with most of the people and goes with a plan or solution where 100% of the people agree.

The approach any unit leader takes is based on a couple of important facts.

The first is how much time does the unit leader have to discuss a situation with others and gain everyone's opinion and vote.
The second is how much expertise do the members of the group have about the problem or situation so the unit leader wants to be more democratic or consensus?

Dr. Mulligan thinks that if unit leaders can transform team members into leaders or specialists in their field, unit leaders can feel more comfortable operating in a more democratic and consensus style of leadership. Thus, he developed the *Triangle Team Leadership Model*: *Becoming the Best in Our Field* so this could happen.

Task Two –Review What Other Professionals Say about Leadership

According to research at the Human Resources Institute of Eckland College in St. Petersburg, Florida, the development of leaders has been a tremendous challenge for companies for the past ten years and will continue to be well into the 21st century. The Human Resources Institute [i] conducted a worldwide study with 312 companies and the results are below.

The Most Important Issues Impacting Organizations in the Next 10 Years

Ranked by Overall Mean Response (n=312)
Key: 1=Extremely Important; 2=Somewhat Important; 3=Important;   4=Not Important

	Overall		*U.S.*		*Europe*		*Asia*	
	Rank	Mean	Rank	Mean	Rank	Mean	Rank	Mean
Information technology	1	1.27	2	1.25	6	1.33	1	1.28
Leadership	2	1.28	1	1.25	9	1.42	5	1.36
Focus on the customer	3	1.29	3	1.28	4	1.27	6	1.36
Skill level of workforce	4	1.34	4	1.35	3	1.21	16	1.56
Managing change	5	1.38	5	1.39	1	2.21	8	1.42
Electronic transfer of info	6	1.43	6	1.46	2	1.21	7	1.38
The information superhighway	7	1.48	7	1.50	5	1.27	9	1.44
Innovation & creativity	8	1.51	8	1.53	10	1.42	12	1.48
Improving productivity	9	1.55	9	1.55	30	1.75	11	1.48
Quality of technical education	10	1.55	13	1.59	16	1.55	4	1.36
Employee communication	11	1.56	10	1.55	20	1.64	20	1.60
Intranet	12	1.59	16	1.61	12	1.46	21	1.60
Enhancing quality	13	1.60	12	1.58	25	1.67	23	2.68
Quality of primary education	14	1.60	11	1.56	28	1.73	32	1.79
Countries' global competitiveness	15	1.64	22	1.74	7	1.38	2	1.32
HR information systems	16	1.65	18	1.68	21	1.64	14	1.52
The learning organization	17	1.66	17	1.64	17	1.61	25	1.75
Quality of higher education	18	1.67	19	1.69	26	1.70	26	1.75
Healthcare costs	19	1.71	15	1.60	61	2.22	40	1.92
Ethics in business	20	1.71	20	1.72	31	1.76	27	1.76
Managing strategic alliances	21	1.75	27	1.81	13	1.50	19	1.60
Rate of economic growth	22	1.77	24	1.78	23	1.67	33	1.83
U.S. competition	23	1.78	14	1.60	38	1.97	75	2.57
Business information software	24	1.78	26	1.80	33	1.79	24	1.72
Quality of work life	25	1.79	28	1.82	24	1.67	29	1.76

The companies in the United States ranked Leadership #1, while European companies ranked Managing Change as #1. Asian companies ranked Information Technology as #1.

An article entitled "The Leadership Industry"[ii] (*Fortune* magazine, Feb. 21, 2008) stated that over 600 institutions offer some formal approach to leadership. In the article, Professor James O' Toole, head of a corporate leadership forum at the Aspen Institute, says, "people were having trouble selling their management ideas under their own labels, so they started calling it leadership." The article also says that Tom Peters, co-author of "In Search of Excellence," is paid $65,000 for speaking one to two hours, or $80,000 a day. A company's willingness to pay such fees illustrates the importance of leadership to today's organizations.

Asking employees what effective leaders do elicits a variety of answers such as:

> ➢ establish the vision or mission ➢ motivate and inspire
> ➢ set a strategy ➢ responsible for results

Still, the definition of effective leadership eludes many organizations.

Warren G. Bennis, educator and author, defines leadership as "the capacity to translate vision into reality." He states that the challenge of leadership is to create a social architecture where ideas, relationships and adventure can flourish. He adds that leaders know who they are; their strengths and weaknesses. They use their strengths and compensate for their weaknesses. They know what they want and why, and how to communicate that in order to gain cooperation and support. Finally, they know how to achieve their goal. Bennis suggests three basic reasons why leaders are important:

1) They are responsible for the effectiveness of the organization

2) They serve as anchors in an organization thus providing stability.

3) They bring integrity to an organization allowing those doing business together to trust one another.

In his book, <u>The Leadership Factor</u>, [iii] John Kotter contends that leadership is the same for a CEO as it is for a project leader ten layers lower in the company. He defines effective leadership as:
1) Setting a change agenda/vision of what can be; a vision which takes into account the legitimate interests of everyone involved.
2) A strategy for achieving the vision that takes into accountant all the organizational and environmental forces.
3). Building a strong implementation network, alliance or coalition powerful enough to implement the strategy.
4). Recruiting/selecting a highly motivated group of influential key people in the network who are committed to making the vision a reality.

Kotter further states "there is a growing need for leadership at all levels. Corporations worldwide are discovering that they need more people who can help them combat the economic warfare created by increased competition. Lower level managerial, professional and technical employees need to play a leadership role in their areas. No matter what the size of a company, it is essential that the CEO have everyone lead in different ways."

What to Look for in Leaders

John Kotter described the following as the requirements needed for providing effective leadership:

1) An inborn need to achieve is motivated by challenge and a strong drive to lead.
2) Strong personal values – a high degree of integrity and honesty.
3) Possessing the ability, skills, keen mind and strong interpersonal skills.
4) An excellent reputation and track record in a broad set of activities.
5) A broad set of solid relationships in the firm and in the industry.
6) Broad knowledge of the industry and company.

Kotter also described the attributes needed in lower and middle management leadership:

- Require an understanding of the position; a broader knowledge than just the technical requirements of the job

- The ability to develop a working relationship with others

- A track record and reputation of being credible

- A minimum set of intellectual and interpersonal skills

- Integrity and honesty

- Minimum energy level and a desire to lead

John Kotter outlined the differences between management and leadership in another book titled, *A Force for Change: How Leadership Differs from Management, 1990.* [iv] Kotter states that management and leadership are not mutually exclusive. A team leader needs to develop the appropriate background and skills to be effective in both areas. A combination of effective leadership and good management can provide structure as well as encourage innovation to bring out the best in everyone. The differences are outlined on the next page.

John Kotter's Overview of Management and Leadership

	Management	*Leadership*
Creating An Agenda	**Planning and Budgeting** Establishing detailed steps and timetables for achieving needed results, and then developing a budget to make it happen	**Establishing Direction** Developing a vision of the future agenda and strategies for producing the changes needed to achieve that vision
Developing A Human Network For Achieving The Agenda	**Organizing and Staffing** Establishing an organization structure for accomplishing results, selecting the right people, delegating authority for carrying out the plan, providing policies and procedures to guide people and creating systems to implement the plans	**Aligning People** Communication the direction by words and deeds to all those whose cooperation may be needed-influencing the creation of teams and coalitions that understand and believe in the vision and strategies and accept their validity
Execution	**Controlling and Problem Solving** Monitoring the step by step plan, making modifications in the plan, and solving problems	**Motivating and Inspiring** Energizing people to overcome obstacles(politics, negatives resource barriers) and meeting unfulfilled human needs
Outcomes	**Obtaining Results** Key to meeting the results that senior management and all the stakeholders want from the company	**Anticipating and Managing Change** Learns what changes the company needs to make to be profitable(new products that customers want, new approaches to labor relations)

Korn Ferry International, a management placement firm, surveyed 1,500 senior leaders [v] in 2006 to describe the key traits needed by CEOs to take them to the year 2015. The four top ingredients necessary for a leader, according to the survey, were:

- Vision
- Strategic skills
- Able to move quickly
- Picking the right individuals to be on the team

The June 21, 2005 *Fortune* magazine [vi] profiled a "Superior CEO" as possessing:

- Integrity, maturity and energy-The foundation on which everything else is built.
- Business acumen-A deep understanding of the business and a strong profit orientation – an almost instinctive feel for how the company makes money.
- People acumen. Judging, leading teams, growing and coaching people; cutting losses where necessary.
- Organization acumen. Engendering trust, sharing information and listening expertly; diagnosing whether the organization is performing at full potential; delivering on commitments; changing, not just running, the business; being decisive and confident.
- Curiosity, intellectual capacity and a global mindset. Being externally oriented and hungry for knowledge of the world; adept at connecting developments and spotting patterns.
- Superior judgment.
- An insatiable appetite for accomplishment and results.
- A powerful motivation to grow and convert learning into practice
- Effective communication skills

Strategic Leadership

- Study the art of directing people: know how to lead, direct, manage.
- Study ahead of them: leadership is drive. Lead by pace setting. Work harder and smarter than your people do. See the problems first and think ahead to solutions.
- Study the art of persuasion: learn how to bring people to your way of thinking. Apply sales psychology in leadership the same as you do in selling.
- Seek your direct reports advice: ask for their opinions. Encourage them to express themselves. Consult with them and accept their ideas. Don't think you know all the angles.
- See their viewpoints: learn to listen to their problems. Hear them out, even when you don't agree. Try to walk in their shoes. Understand before you decide.
- Help them to see your viewpoint: explain your point of view better, don't just state it. Justify and support it. Give your reasons. The will help you and cooperate more readily if they know the background and reasons for your decision.
- Get the job done well: follow through on plans. Hold meetings often and regularly.
- Face unpleasantness frankly: air troubles. Have bull sessions when necessary. Permit and encourage suggestions when things aren't going smoothly.

What Derails Leaders

M. W. McCall, Jr., and M. M. Lombardo [vii] wrote a technical report in June 2003 entitled, "Off the Track: Why and How Successful Executives Get Derailed." The authors stated that executives get derailed because of the following ten fatal flaws:

1) Specific performance problems with the business – this person can't handle certain parts of the business and fails to admit the problem. He or she covers it up, blames others and shows that they can't change.

2) Insensitivity to others – an abrasive, intimidating, bully-style of behavior.

3) Cold, aloof and arrogant – some managers are so brilliant that they become arrogant and intimidate others with their knowledge. This type of person is criticized because he/she makes others feel stupid, doesn't listen, has all the answers.

4) Betrayal of trust – this is where a manager commits what is perhaps a manager's only forgivable sin. They betray a trust. Some people use information about others as power and use it for their own good. The failure to follow through on promises also creates havoc

5) Over managing – failing to delegate, empower or build a team that can handle operational activities. At the executive level, it is fatal because you have a staff of self-managers who want to be in charge, having full authority to run their own area.

6) Overly ambitious – thinking of the next job, playing politics. People bruise others and spend too much time pleasing upper management.

7) Failing to staff effectively – some managers get along with their staff but have the wrong people in the job. They staff in their own image and don't release people quickly enough when they perform poorly.

8) Inability to think strategically – preoccupied with detail and don't see the big picture. They can't go from being doers to being planners.

9) Unable to adapt to a boss with a different style. This situation can cause a person to get into wars over differences, fight problems with opinions and not facts and let the issues get personal.

10) Over-dependence on a mentor or advocate. Sometimes individuals stay with a single advocate or mentor too long. When the mentor falls, so do you.

Twenty-One Suggestions for People Who Want to Lead

1) Let each person know what to expect and where they stand; do not fail to discuss their performance with them periodically.

2) Give credit where credit is due; commensurate with accomplishments.

3) Inform people of changes in advance. Informed people are more effective.

4) Let people participate in plans and decisions affecting them.

5) Gain your people's confidence; earn their loyalty and trust.

6) Know all your people personally. Find out their interests, habits and touchy points.

7) Listen to your subordinate's proposals. They have good ideas too.

8) If a person's behavior is unusual for him/her, find out why. There is always a reason.

9) Try to make your wishes known by suggestion or request when ever possible. People generally don't like to be pushed.

10) Explain why things are to be done. People will do a better job when they know the reason for something.

11) When you make a mistake, admit it and apologize. Others will resent your blaming someone else.

12) Show people the importance of every job. It will satisfy their need to belong.

13) Criticize constructively. Give reasons for your criticism and suggest ways in which performance can be improved.

14) Precede criticisms with mention of a person's good points; show you are trying to help.

15) Do as you would have your people do. The leader sets the example.

16) Be consistent in your actions; let your people have little doubt as to what is expected.

17) Take every opportunity to demonstrate pride in the group-bring out the best in them.

18) If one person gripes, find out his grievance. One person's gripe may be the gripe of many.

19) Settle every grievance if at all possible; otherwise the whole group will be affected.

20) Set short and long-range goals by which people can measure their progress.

21) Back-up your people. Authority must be given when people are ready for it. [viii]

Task Three- Learn Why We Need Effective Team Unit Leaders.

Yesterday,

Prior to the middle 80's, companies did not face the competitive challenges of today's organizations. The majority of workers stayed with one company most of their career. They depended on the organization to take care of them through the work years and into retirement. Long-term strategies and succession planning were consistently part of the business agenda as multi-layers of team unit leaders positions existed offering excellent advancement opportunities for everyone. Change was slow and anxiety was low.

Today

More than at any time in history, we are living in an age of change. Major changes in our lives are more rapid, complex, turbulent and unpredictable; they are unlike any changes we have encountered before. We are in an era that is sweeping society into a massive transformation that will have a lasting effect on the workplace. It is estimated that there have been more structural changes in U.S. industry in the last five years than in the previous thirty. Continuous change, complexity, constraints and conflicts best characterize today's business environment. Major economic, technological, social, cultural and political forces are driving the way firms do business and how they position their resources. Four million workers are leaving their companies monthly because of change.

One of the biggest challenges facing CEOs and team unit leaders is anticipating and managing change. Executives and managers are constantly talking about how to adjust to fast-moving change, charting, comprehending and overcoming them. Oakleigh Thorne, Chief Executive Officer of C.C.H., Inc. was quoted in *The Chicago Tribune* as saying:

> "The pace of change is so fast today that if you don't have your
> antenna up and aren't modifying your plans to react to the change,
> you are dead. Change is certain, progress is not."

New patterns of interdependence among governments, companies, unions, managers and workers are emerging, as we have become a world community. The work sector has become a playing field without borders.

Of all the changes, the one that has affected industry sectors the most is **the pressure to generate higher earnings to increase shareholder value** in the publicly held stock companies. The daily stock market report is the most important news of the day. People who invest in companies want to know how their investment is doing. This pressure to increase shareholder value has forced publicly held stock companies to find locations where they pay less taxes. When this happens, it hurts the amount of money given to the federal, state and local governments and reduces the amount of money given to nonprofit organizations. This has impacted employment in all sectors.

14

The importance of increasing shareholder value has also forced the National Association of Corporate Directors to issue new guidelines. The association is making it clear that senior executives should serve on no more than one or two boards besides their own and retired executives no more than six. Guidelines also state that employers should not have inattentive, passive and uninformed people serving on their board. Companies are paying directors with more stock and less cash. The change in compensation and the emphasis on accountability has caused board members to put the heat on the senior management team like never before.

The marching orders for CEOs and presidents of publicly held stock companies are simple — hit your profit targets or be gone. In essence, making money and satisfying stockholders today has become the number one priority. One executive said to Dr. Mulligan "Our company has had five presidents in six years." A recent *Chicago Tribune* issue revealed the average time for a CEO in a Fortune 500 company is now two and one-half years. Many foreign companies who have bought American companies only want one thing – a high return on investment.

Private companies strive to make profit just as publicly held stock organizations. If your company is profitable, you can obtain more money when you sell your organization. Secondly, if you have excellent cash flow and profit, you can be more competitive by attracting and retaining talented employees and gain market share acquiring companies.

The enormous pressure to increase earnings has forced many CEOs, presidents and senior management teams to take action steps that leaders in the earlier years never contemplated. The challenge of raising the company stock value has pushed organizations to implement tough and difficult strategies. Some of these have included:
- Downsizing, restructuring and reengineering the workforce on a large scale.
- Continuously rightsizing on a small scale.
- Using advanced technology to do more work with fewer people.
- Eliminating specific positions and asking those remaining to take on more responsibility, work longer hours and do more with fewer resources.
- Outsourcing specific department areas such as IT, benefits, etc.
- Eliminating the cost of benefits by hiring more temporary and part time people.
- Issuing contracts to large national providers instead of local small businesses
- Acquiring or merging with other companies to increase sales and market share, and position the company as a leader in the industry.
- Moving manufacturing off shore to obtain less expensive labor.
- Moving away from research, development and manufacturing to find products produced by others.
- Tightening control on expenses to come in below budget.
- Taking longer to pay suppliers and vendors.
- Making the retired/present employees pay more for their benefits and retire early

In many cases, these management strategies have driven stock prices up but they have also created havoc within the workforce, causing such problems as:

- Anger (a feeling of being used and not appreciated)
- Insecurity (fear of job loss)
- Distrust (poor working relationship)
- Lack of focus (productivity)
- Organization paranoia (we vs. they)
- Low morale (attitudes)
- Poor performance (meeting expectations)
- No commitment (purpose)
- Sickness (absenteeism)
- Fear of job loss (high anxiety)
- Burn-out (distress)
- Feeling of abandonment (analytic depression)
- Not being able to think and solve problems (stress/tension)
- Inability to learn complex material (distraction)
- A lack of loyalty (retention)
- A loss of experienced people (early retirement)

Workers who feel less secure in their jobs are also more likely to be less loyal to their companies and will be sending out their resumes. Hot jobs.com stated 50% of workers plan to leave their company by the end of 2012. Search firms know which companies are in trouble when they receive dozens of resumes from people in the same organization.

The elimination of team unit leaders in companies has compounded the problem. The loss of effective coaches (managers and supervisors) has impacted employee engagement performance and retention. Business places less value on management training while sports places top value on their coaching staff. The recent escalation of coaching salaries in professional sports illustrates the value placed on the development of people or the players.

In essence, people have always been considered a company's most important asset. However, if you don't pay attention to the people who help you succeed, they can turn out to be your greatest liability. As one candidate in an outplacement program said, "My company practiced the mushroom management style. They constantly left us in the dark and continued to feed us more manure."

Although senior management is under enormous pressure to produce earnings, they cannot forget the people who will get them there. The best coached and most cohesive teams will win championships and be the top company in their industry.

Tomorrow's Challenge- *To Develop Team Unit Leaders into Highly Effective Leaders, Managers, Mentors and Provide Them with A Performance Management System That Will Help Them Build Champion Performers and Championship Teams Throughout the Organization.*

As CEOs, presidents and senior management continue to have the pressure of increasing profit each year, they must have a stable, cohesive, well prepared, focused, committed and competitive workforce behind them. This means they must find and develop the best team unit leaders and managers in their industry. In the long run, it is the team unit leaders (counseling and coaching staff) who will make the difference in growing people and the company.

If your team unit leaders:

- Treat direct reports equally as important as customers and shareholders,
- Ask direct reports to engage in the planning process and develop the objectives that need to be achieved,
- Excite direct reports about the vision, mission and objectives of their department and company,
- Can work with direct reports so they achieve individual, team unit and company champion building objectives,
- Help direct reports feel like they are growing as a leader in their field and contributing to the profitability and advancement of the organization,
- Develop direct reports into high-level performers, leaders, problem solvers, and empower them,
- Treat direct reports like they belong,
- Make work meaningful for direct reports,
- Teach direct reports how to manage stress and be healthy,
- Can help direct reports in career development and advancement,
- Help direct reports balance their lives,
- Recognize and reward direct reports for their performance,
- Can operate as effective One-On-One Idiosyncratic Managers so you retain more employees,
- Can generate pride, enthusiasm and partnerships (PEP) in all employees

You will create an organization that has loyal and committed employees and a company that will become and be the best in it's industry.

If you don't know where you are going, you might end up some place where you do not want to be.

A Homeless Person

Step Two

Review the Importance of Business Planning, the Gap Analysis and Closure Model and Task Empowerment Process

We would like you to complete the following *three tasks* to complete *Step Three*.

Page

19

Task One- Review the Importance of Developing a Business Plan

Dr. Mulligan invested some money once in a company that was growing shrimp in a factory setting. All investors were suppose to make 100 times their investment. Dr. Mulligan made the mistake of giving the company some money before he had read their business plan. It was like you were lucky to know someone to get in on this deal. When Dr. Mulligan was asked to be on their Board, he discovered they had no in-depth business plan. The individuals running the show thought if they could grow large numbers of shrimp in an indoor facility, they could sell the process for 60 million. Some things went wrong and they ran out of cash. They had no solid business plan and a potential business failed.

We would like you to review the following seven stages of developing a business plan.

Stage One-   **Definitions**
Stage Two-   **The Purpose and Need for Planning**
Stage Three- **Why Many Team Unit Leaders Do Not Plan**
Stage Four-   **The Characteristics of Good Planning**
Stage Five-   **Steps In the Planning Process**
Stage Six-   **Organization Wide-Planning**
Stage Seven- **Developing a Budget-Chart of Accounts**

Stage One-Definitions

1) **Performance** is defined as setting an objective and displaying certain behaviors and performing specific tasks to achieve the objective with in a written timeline (a starting and ending time). The objective has to be measurable.

2) **Managing** is establishing objectives, a plan and budget and organizing, directing, coordinating and controlling people and the situations to achieve the objectives.

3) A **system** is a process (step by step approach) in managing people, time, a budget and achieving the agreed upon objectives.

4) **Planning** is the process by which an organization can become what it wants to become.

5) **Planning** is the identification of opportunity and the allocation of resources to exploit the opportunity.

6) **Planning** is the rational determination of where you are, where you want to go and how and when you are going to get there.

7) A **plan** is a narrative statement describing an action program – who is to do what and when to achieve an objective.

8) A **budget** is not a plan. The budget identifies the revenue and expense stream expected as the result of an action program. The budget is monitored daily, weekly, and monthly to determine where you are financially. Cash flow is important to an organization staying in business.

9) **Strategic planning** is the determination of what products or services are to be offered to what class or classes of customers in what geographical area – what business or businesses you are going to be in this year, next year and five years from now.

10) **Operational planning** is the determination as to how to run the present business or businesses most effectively in the period immediately ahead.

Stage Two-*The Purpose and Need for Planning*

1) *Planning* is carried out to determine what must be accomplished today, this week, this month or this year so that the organization will be in a satisfactory situation next month, next year or five years hence.

2) *Planning* is not concerned with future decisions but with the future impact of present decisions.

3) *Planning* jumps ahead to the end of the time period under consideration and works back to determine what should be accomplished at intervals in time, and specifically, what actions should be taken now to maximize the probability that the objectives for the period will be attained.

4) *Planning* is not intended to eliminate risks – risk is essential to progress – but to assure that the right risks are taken at the right time.

5) *Planning* is intended to insure the most effective use of available resources toward the attainment of the most important objectives.

6) *Planning* is intended to minimize the number of crises which must be handled on an emergency basis – with managers focusing on crisis prevention rather than crisis solving.

7) *Strategic planning* is ordinarily done by relatively few people at the top of the organization with the personal involvement of the *Chief Executive Officer*.

8) *Strategic planning* involves at least one to three years ahead. Usually the limiting factor is the quantity and the quality of managerial competence.

9) *Operational planning* should involve every team unit leader/manager in the organization and is normally, but not necessarily, tied to the fiscal year.

10) Some examples of *planning* are illustrated below.
   - In a construction company, most operational planning is done on a project basis.
   - A highly seasonal retail business might have an operational plan for each selling season.
   - A capital goods company with a long order cycle may plan on an 18 or 24 month basis.
   - Some aspects of an operational plan may have a long time cycle, i.e., a timber company may plant trees which won't be harvested for 50 years.

21

A Need for Planning Continued

In an environment of accelerating change, the management of change is both the challenge and the opportunity.

1) We must plan for an uncertain future.
- The future will not be an extension of the past – and it will be different from the present.
- The rate of change will continue to accelerate.

2) We must plan in the midst of concurrent revolutions.
- The rate of technological progress is accelerating – bringing "discontinuous" change.
- Population is rapidly changing in number, age, location, education and degree of affluence.
- Expectations are rising sharply – all people see the material benefits of a "good" life – and want it now.
- Increasingly, individuals (particularly the ablest individuals) are interested in and motivated by considerations other than money alone.

3) The economic life of managerial decisions is shortened while the cost of decisions is increasing.
- On the average, a product has a profitable life of less than six to eight years.
- On the average, a new product reaches maximum volume within two years after it reaches one-tenth of maximum volume.
- On the average, the time from "invention" or technical breakthrough to commercial application is now less than five years.

4) The size and complexity of organizations, per se, requires more effective planning for coordination and control.
- Team unit leaders are supposed to make good things happen which would not otherwise have happened – what's different and better this year in your area of responsibility because you planned it that way.
- Good results without good planning come from good luck rather than good management.
- The objective of planning is not the development of "a plan" but the establishment of an ongoing planning process as a routine part of management.
- Every manager has a planning responsibility at three levels:
  - ✓ To lead the planning in his/her own area of responsibility.
  - ✓ To coordinate his/her planning with the planning being done by other managers whose responsibilities are interrelated.
  - ✓ To contribute to the development of the organization-wide plan.

Stage Three- *Why Many Managers Do Not Like To Plan*

1) It Takes Time

- Planning is a time-generating activity but requires an initial investment of time.
- We don't have time to plan this week or this month, primarily because we didn't plan well enough last week, last month or last year.

2) It Involves Thought – The Hardest Work We Do

- Some team unit leaders consciously or unconsciously keep themselves busy on the parts of their job responsibilities they like to do or know they do well to avoid   facing up to the part of their job which is more difficult or with which they are less familiar.

3) It Involves Paperwork or to be Recorded – Every Plan Should Be Reduced To Writing

- The discipline or reducing a plan to writing usually improves the quality of the plan.
- The plan must be recorded as a baseline for the operation of a system of control.

4) Organization-wide planning requires individual team unit leaders to adhere to some systematic procedure – a plan and time schedule for planning

5) Involvement in planning usually ends with commitment to a specific result on a specific time schedule

- Some team unit leaders do not want to be committed because:

    ✓ If there are no objectives, one can never fail.
    ✓ If there is no destination, one can never be lost.

Stage Four-*The Characteristics of Good Planning*

1) **Objective Oriented**
- **Early in the planning process, objectives are tentatively identified and the rest of the planning process is directed to the development of an action program for attainment of the objectives.**
- **Objectives are initially subjectively determined and ought not to be frozen until an action program, which makes their attainment probable, has been developed.**

2) **Factually Based**
- **Results are attained outside of the organization.**
- **Current information as to the attitudes, problems, interests, expectations of customers or prospective customers ought to be fed into the planning process.**

3) **Assumptions Identified**
- **The uncontrollable factors which have an impact on the organization should be identified.**
- **Using all information which can reasonably be obtained, plus the best judgment available, judgments or assumptions should be made and recorded as to the expected situation in respect to each one of the uncontrollable factors.**

4) **Involves Subordinates**
- **Members of the team other than the manager usually have information, experience, imagination and creativity which will make a contribution to the plan.**
- **The commitment of subordinates to the achievement of the plan is in direct proportion to their degree of involvement in the development of the program.**

5) Assigns Tasks and Times
- **Everything which needs to be done must be assigned to a specific individual on a specific time schedule.**

6) Provides for Control
- **Every plan should be broken into time segments as a basis for control.**

7) Periodic Review and Rework
- **The plan should be monitored and reviewed periodically to determine whether all the things which are supposed to be done have in fact been done**

8) Make Things Happen
- **Planning which does not bring result has been solely an intellectual exercise.**

Stage Five- *Steps in the Planning Process*

For Senior Management and Team Unit Leaders
   A. The Present Situation – Where Are You Now?

1) **What business or businesses are you in today**
   (The definition should be broad enough to stimulate thinking and to provide opportunity for innovation and growth, but narrow enough to provide direction and channel thinking.)

2) **What are the critical factors (sales, profits, turnover, rejects, machine downtime, etc.) and for each critical factor, what is the trend?**

3) **What are the major strengths that will provide a basis for progress?**

4) **What are the major weaknesses which would be barriers to progress if nothing is done to correct them? Over time, the limiting factor to success is normally the quantity and quality of managerial competence.**

5) **Where will you be in two to five years if you continue doing just what you are doing today?**

   B. What are the Assumptions with Respect to the Uncontrollable Factors in the Environment?

Ordinarily, this is the most difficult part of planning – planning requires that we determine what can be accomplished and how we will operate in a period of the future, where we will be affected by factors which we cannot control or even foresee.

These factors should be identified and, using whatever information can be reasonably collected, plus judgment, an assumption is made about each factor.

Assumptions fall into four broad categories:

- *Economic:* Gross national product – construction expenditures – disposable income – interest rates, inflation, etc.
- *Social:* Leisure time – buying habits – customer attitudes – demographic factors, etc.
- *Governmental*: Taxes – exchange controls – import controls – wage or price controls, etc.
- *Competitive:* Changes in product – prices – policies, services, etc.

C. What are the Objectives – Where Do You Want to be at the End of the Time Period?

1) Objectives, to be useful in management, must be measurable.

2) Objectives must be challenging – people do better with appropriate challenge.

3) Objectives must be realistic and attainable – success breeds success and failure breeds failure – a pattern of failure de-motivates.

- Three to five year objectives can be set at a level that can not be reached by the present people with knowledge, skill and experience being developed.

- Short-range (one year or less) objectives must be set in relation to the present capability of the people.

1) Objectives must be acceptable – you must be willing to commit resources and to pay the price.

2) Objectives must be compatible with each other or an established priority.

D. What are the Alternative Programs Which Might Lead to the Attainment of the Objectives?

The process ought to attempt to maximize innovation and creativity.

1) Good ideas are not limited to a few people in an organization, nor are they related directly to a degree or education or position in the organization, or even to intelligence. They may be anywhere in the organization.

2) Creativity is maximized in a pressure situation where the objectives are precisely defined and everyone is pushed to come up with ideas. These ideas are focused on the attainment of the objectives on the basis that if the suggestions are made now, they will truly be considered.

3) It is easy to turn off creativity. Avoid negative reactions, especially ridicule.

4) It is no accident that many of the great breakthroughs came from outside an existing industry – everyone in the industry already knew what could not be done.

E. The Decision Process

1) For each alternative, estimate the probability of success – this is a subjective judgment.

2) For each alternative, estimate the probable cost.

3) Select the alternatives with the most favorable cost-probability situations.

4) Determine the degree of commitment obtainable for each alternative – a second rate program to which people are really committed may have a better chance of success than a first rate program imposed on people.

5) The implementation of a decision requires a clear and specific commitment from each individual involved, to the effect that one:
   - Knows his/her responsibilities.
   - Knows the results desired.
   - Accepts consequences for actions
   - Knows when the actions are to be taken and completed.
   - Can and will be accountable in achieving the desired result.

F. Establish a Review or Control Procedure

This consists of subdividing the plan in time so that there are clear and precise checkpoints at intervals to determine whether the program is on target.

1) Ordinarily an annual plan should be broken down into quarters.

2) Any review must look to actions taken or completed and not just to comparison or operating figures with budget figures. The actions that are not taken by top managers do not ordinarily show up in budget comparisons for three to six months.

G. Review and Rework

There should be a periodic review.

1) Is a major assumption no longer valid? In this case, perhaps the plan should be totally revised in the light of unexpected external conditions. Are the assumptions still valid? If so, the burden to develop a catch-up program is on the responsible individual.

2) Every significant unfavorable deviation from the plan should require the development and implementation of an action program – more managers fail because they do nothing than because they do something wrong

Stage *Six- Organization Wide Planning*

A. The continuous interest, support and participation of the CEO.

B. The assignment of specific planning responsibility to an individual (a Director of Planning Coordination) who facilitates the planning. He/she must:

- Develop a plan for planning (who must do what, when to develop an organization-wide plan)
- Give guidelines and assistance to team unit leaders.
- Bring together departmental, and divisional team unit leaders to be sure that such plans are compatible.
- Be sure that each team unit plan includes a compatible budget.
- Be sure that the organization-wide plan is broken down into compatible marketing, manufacturing, engineering, personnel and product development programs and to divisional and departmental programs where appropriate.
- Be sure that checkpoints exist for the continuous monitoring of the plan.

What questions do you have about planning?

Stage Seven- Use a Chart of Accounts to Establish Your Budget

The following is a chart of accounts to help you develop a budget. It is important to develop a budget because it tells you how much money you need to bring in to pay for your expenses and what your total expenses will be to run your business Obviously, if you are not bringing in enough money from sales or elsewhere to pay your expenses, you need to cut your expenses somewhere. Your budget acts as your compass helping you move forward to make profit and be successful.

Chart of Accounts Income   **January 1 to December 30**
1015- Sales- Income
1016 Common Stock
1017- Interest Income
1018- Loan from Owners

Chart of Accounts-Expense
1101-Checking-Cash
1165-Office Furniture
1166-Computer Equipment
1176- Accumulative. Depreciation of Computers
1198- Organization Expense
1212- Accounts Payable
1202- American Express Payments
1232- Accrued and Withholding
1234-State Withheld
1237- Advancements from Officers
1271- 5940- Travel
1283- Retained earnings
3000- Open Balance Equity
5020- Salaries-Officers-
5100- Advertising
5110- Automobile Expense
5160-Bank Service Charges
5270- Computer Expense
5280- Credit Card Payments
5290- Delivery
5340- Depreciation Expense
5350- Contributions
5360- Dues and Subscriptions
5370- Education and Seminars
5550- Legal and Accounting
5375- Equipment Lease

Chart of Accounts Continued

5390- Entertainment
5410- Gifts
5440- Insurance, General, Auto, Disability, Health
5443- Insurance, Life
5510- Interest Expense
5600- Medical Reimbursement
5605- Miscellaneous Expense
5630- Office Supplies
5650- Outside Service
5670- Pension and Profit Sharing
5675- Petty Cash
5680- Postage
5720- Printing
5725- Professional Services
5730- Rent-Office
5735- Rent-Equipment
5740- Repairs and Maintenance
5790- Storage
5800- Taxes General
5820- Taxes-FICA Expense
5880- Taxes-State
5890- Taxes-Federal
5920- Telephone
5930- Testing Supplies
9800-Websites
9920- State Income Tax
9910- Federal Income Tax

You can break down your sales chart accounts by products and services to learn where your income is being generated.

Task Two- Review the *Gap Analysis & Closure Model*

The GAP Analysis & Closure Model was developed to help you determine where you are, now, where you want to be and how you will get there. Team units, team members and team unit leaders must start off by identifying what their "best in our field" objectives are going to be and then use this process to analyze how they are going to move from Point A to Point B and close this *Gap*. Let's use increasing organization income as an example.

THE GAP ANALYSIS & CLOSURE PROCESS:

Step 1:   We will increase our total income from \$_____ to \$_____ in 201_____..
Our *Gap* includes where our total income is at the beginning of the year versus where we want our income to be at the end of the year. The task is identifying and executing programs that will generate more income that will close the *Gap*.

Step 2:   We will analyze and identify the programs that we have in place that generate income. We will identify the best revenue generators and the ones that are our least revenue generators.

Step 3:   We will analyze each program further and determine which ones we keep, the ones we drop, the ones we modify and any new programs that we need to put in place to increase our income from \$_____ to \$_____ in 201_____.

Step 4:   We will use the *Gap Analysis and Closure Process* for each income generating program. We will develop an income and budget objective for each program and identify the tasks we need to execute to help the program be successful.

Step 5:   After we identify the six income producing programs that will close the *Gap* of where we are now and want to be at the end of the year, we need to monitor each program so it meets it's income and budget objective. If these six programs don't meet their income and budget objective, the chances are reduced that we will close the *Gap* and meet our total income objective .

Step 6:   We will use the *Gap Analysis and Closure Model* to analyze each income generating program. We will identify the tasks we need to execute and complete to meet the predetermined income and budget objective.

Step 7:   We need to identify who is accountable for executing the *Gap Analysis & Closure Model* for each income generating program and work with that person.

Step 8:   Each unit leader will use the *Task Empowerment Process* to meet objectives and close the designated *Gap* of each program (see next page).

"Skill and Confidence are an Unconquered Army"

George Herbert

Task Three-Review the *Task Empowerment Process*

(A Five Step Process)

The *Task Empower Process* is a process that unit leaders can use in One-On-One sessions to help their direct reports establish and execute tasks to meet objectives (challenges). This <u>five step</u> program is meant to help individuals execute all their assigned tasks in an expert manner so the gaps in the *Gap Analysis & Closure System* are closed or the objectives are met by the dates that were established.

In the *first step*, the unit leader and direct reports identify the tasks that need to be met to help achieve a specific objective in the *Gap Analysis & Closure Model*.

In the *second step*, the direct report and unit leader identifies the tasks where coaching is needed and those tasks that he/she can do alone.

In the *third step*, the Team Unit Leader empowers the direct report to perform the tasks that he/she can do alone to meet the objective.

In the *fourth step*, the Team Unit Leader will coach the direct report on identified tasks where he/she needs coaching.

In the *fifth step*, the direct report is empowered to perform the remaining tasks. This means the direct report at this time is an expert in performing all the tasks that have been assigned to him/her and should be able to meet his/her objectives and help the unit meet it's objectives.

Some tasks are related to closing deals to bring in sales or income. The Team Unit Leader should make it clear when the direct report should execute the task alone or bring in more fire power to close the deal.

33

The Triangle Team Leadership Model: Becoming the Best

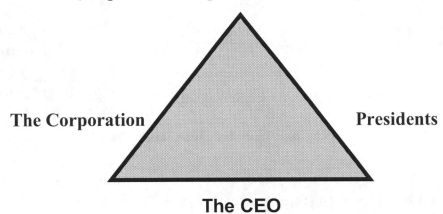

(Corporate Triangle Team Leadership Model)

The Corporation | Presidents

The CEO

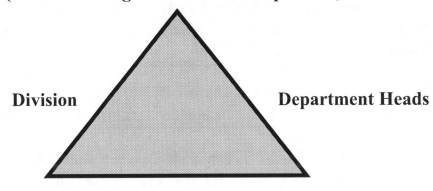

(Division Triangle Team Leadership Model)

Division | Department Heads

Division President

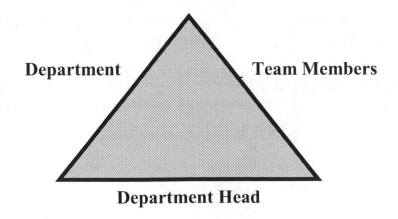

(Department Triangle Team Leadership Model)

Department | Team Members

Department Head

Step Three-

Learn and Execute the Triangle Team Leadership Model: Becoming the Best in Our Field, a leadership and performance management model

We would like you to complete the following *four tasks* to complete *Step Four*.

Page

Task One- Review the Need for This Model, the Thinking Behind the Model and an Outline of the Model

The Need-As CEOs and their senior management team continue to have the pressure of meeting their objectives each year, they must build and maintain a workforce that is and continues to be the best in their field. However, with continuous downsizing and restructuring, the task of retaining a workforce that is capable of achieving the yearly objectives can become increasingly more difficult to accomplish. When changes are not properly managed, a neurotic and unfocused workforce can emerge. The six-letter word "change" can become a five-letter world called "chaos".

The continued change of team leaders, pressure placed on everyone to do more, lack of communication and cooperation and the loss of colleagues can cause employees to feel insecure, abandoned, angry and fearful of losing their job. If negativity starts to escalate, loyalty, productivity, performance and profit will decline. Top performers will then start to jump to a secure place because they don't want to be on a sinking ship.

The push year after year to increase earnings per share and to drive up the stock prices or meet other objectives can take its toll on a workforce and eventually drown a company. We must consider the lessons of the Titanic, an unsinkable ship that drowned in the depths of the Atlantic because its owner and investor pressed the captain to forge ahead at full speed. Fame and fortune fueled their desire to make record time to New York, yet had safety and a steady speed been top priorities, 1500 tragic deaths could have been avoided. Organizations must keep in mind the needs and wants of everyone on the boat and not just the few occupying the executive suites.

CEO's and the senior management team must develop and implement a performance management system that will benefit all stakeholders and put the company on track to become and continually be a championship organization. Phil Jackson, former head coach of the Chicago Bulls, put together the *Triangle Offense*, a coaching philosophy and system that won nine NBA Championships. Bill Walsh, the head coach of the San Francisco 49ers, won three Super Bowls in the 1990s. He developed a system that was known as the *West Coast Offense*. Mike Holmgren and Mike Shanahan, who worked under Bill Walsh later became head NFL coaches using this system to win Super Bowls. There are 12 other people who are NFL head coaches who worked under Bill Walsh. Being part of a winning organization is not only profitable but advances careers.

The June 1999 issue of *Fortune Magazine* [x] stated that General Electric's Jack Welch's strategy is spot people early, follow them, grow them, and stretch them in jobs of increasing complexity. The article quoted Welch as saying, "we spend all our time on people. The day we screw up the people thing, this company is over." Mr. Welch received volumes of information on his people, both good and bad, from multiple sources. Welch and his senior team tracked executives' progress in detail through a system of regular reviews. His written feedback to subordinates was specific, constructive and to the point.

Welch continually evaluated the beliefs of high-level executives aligned with the organization's core values. If the executives weren't on board, GE was not the place for them. This continual pruning and nurturing of people gave GE a powerful competitive advantage few companies understood and achieved. This was known as the extraordinary longevity of top executives system, or *putting people first and strategy second.*

When you study leaders who are at the top in their industry or field, you will discover that they all have a leadership development and performance management system in place that can transform people and their teams into champions. A model winning system can take individuals and teams to the top, serving as a guide for everyone to follow.

The Thinking Behind the Model-The *Triangle Team Leadership Model: Becoming the Best in Our Field* was designed by Dr. Michael V. Mulligan to help CEOs and their team unit leaders transform direct reports into champion performers (leaders in their fields) and the team units and company into championship/profitable organizations. This *Model* can be used not only by business executives but by coaches who manage sports teams and on college campuses by resident advisors in residence halls and by officers in fraternities and sororities who want to help others grow.

The two key factors to this system include the performance of direct reports and the team unit leader. The first key is that individual employees have to set and perform tasks to meet specific objectives that will help their team unit, division and corporation meet their champion building objectives. If employees establish and achieve champion building objectives that are both company and personal growth focused, they will not only help the company be successful but they will grow into an expert task leader or champion performer in their field. The second key to the system, and an extremely important one, is how the team unit leader directs, motivates, and helps his/her direct reports set and achieve these champion building objectives

Dr. Mulligan gained many ideas for developing the system through his educational and work-related experience. He served as management development director for the largest franchise in North America and was a One-On-One Career Coach to 2,500 plus executives.

Dr. Mulligan liked what Dr. John Kotter had to say about leadership and management and created the *Triangle Team Leadership Model* taking into account his four main points.
- Team unit leaders should establish a vision and mission statement and growth objectives that take into account the legitimate interest of all stakeholders.
- Strategies and a plan should be established to help achieve the vision and mission and growth objectives and take into account organization forces and impediments.
- A strong performance partnership network system should be established to implement the business plan and strategies to achieve the objectives.
- Recruit and select a highly motivated group of influential key team unit leaders who are committed to achieving the growth objectives to advance people & unit.

An Outline of the Model-The company, depending on it's size, needs to develop a strategy on how to execute the *Model*. A small size organization that has no divisions could call the process the *Double Triangle Team Leadership Model* (Company and Departments). A large organization could integrate three triangle team leadership partnerships into one system and they could call it their *Triple Triangle Team Leadership Model*.

#1 The Corporate Triangle Team Leadership Model: Becoming the Best in Our Field

The **first triangle in the triple system** would include the CEO, the Corporation (board members) and division team unit leaders (presidents of the divisions). The CEO and division presidents would develop a motivating vision and mission statement, growth objectives and a business plan with strategies and a budget for the corporation. This group then selects and monitors the team unit leaders (department heads) both at the corporate office and the divisions. The CEO and division presidents develop the corporate growth objectives and then develops their personal growth objectives that tie into helping the corporation and themselves be successful. See organizational structure below.

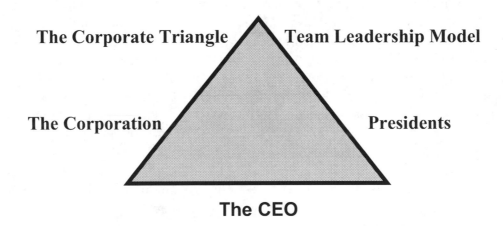

Afterwards, the CEO meets with the division presidents One- On- One to monitor and measure their progress and coach them where needed. He/she can use the Task Empowerment Process if needed but has to be careful not to insult his/her division presidents. The Board monitors and measures the results of the CEO. This book can be used by the CEO when working with the division presidents. The CEO will work closely with The Performance Evaluation Committee, the group that will coordinate, monitor and measure the results of the company, divisions, departments and individuals. The CEO and division presidents and department heads can go on line to see how every team unit is doing. Individuals who are not team unit leaders can go on line to learn how they are doing as an individual as well as their team unit. Individual reports should be reviewed by the individual and his/her boss.

#2 The Division Triangle Team Leadership Model: Becoming the Best in Our Field

The **second triangle** includes the division president, the division and department heads. The division president reveals the corporate vision and mission statements, growth objectives and business plan. The President and department heads discuss the corporate vision, mission, growth objectives and business plan as it relates to their division. The division can develop their own vision and mission statements, growth objectives, action plans and strategies, budget and monitoring/measuring process to make their division a championship organization. The division president and department heads identify the growth objectives that their department and division must meet to be successful and have themselves be rated as leaders in their field and champion performers.

The Division Triangle Team Leadership Model

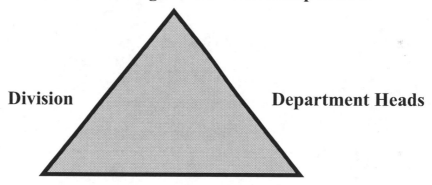

Division   Department Heads

Division President

The division president meets one- on -one with each department head and monitors and measures their progress. The President empowers the department heads and counsels, advises and coaches them using the *Task Empowerment Process*. This work book by Dr. Mulligan can be used by department heads when the division presidents are working with them. The division presidents will work report directly to the Performance Evaluation Committee, the committee established to monitor the system and rate everyone.

#3 Department Triangle Team Leadership Model: Becoming the Best in Our Field

The **third triangle** includes the department head, the department itself and direct reports. The department head shares with his/her direct reports the vision and mission statements, growth objectives, business plan and strategies and budget of the division and corporation. The department partnership then develops their own vision and mission statements, growth objectives, business plan and strategies that need to be achieved to help the Corporation and division achieve their objectives. The department needs to meet it's champion building objectives to be rated a championship team and best in the field.

The Department Triangle Team Leadership Model

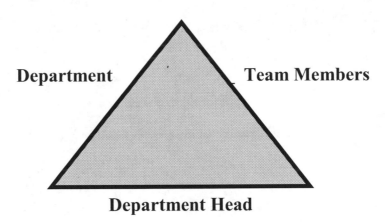

Department   Team Members

Department Head

The Department Head meets with team members One-On-One to monitor and measure their progress using *The Task Empowerment Process*. The Department Head asks each team member to establish their own growth objectives and tie many of them into helping the department, division and corporation meet their objectives. The Department Head should counsel, advise and coach each team member so they meet their stated objectives and are rated an expert leader in their field. A supplement book titled *The Team Members' Plans* was developed to help Department Heads implement The *Triangle Leadership by Objectives Model* with their direct reports. The unit leader can call 847 981-5725 to order books for their direct reports.

Employees at this level are definitely motivated in making money but they are also interested in their career development and advancement. The senior management team, although interested in their careers, are more interested in driving up the company stock price because they usually have more shares in the company.

The key to achieving the corporate and division business objectives depends on the departments meeting their objectives. John Kotter made the point clear that if senior team leaders are to be successful, they must develop a network of team unit leaders who will implement strategies beneficial to all stakeholders. There should be team unit leaders throughout the organization who are committed and prepared to meet the growth objectives.

The June 21, 2009 issue of *Fortune* magazine reinforced Kotter's message by saying that 70% of CEOs fail because they don't have an adequate team leadership system in place to execute the strategic plan. In essence, CEOs need to have a competitive network of team unit leaders to help them execute and achieve their plan. Every person who manages others should be a part of this network. A chain of command needs to be established to build a strong chain/organization with no weak links.

Many CEOs seem convinced that their communication carries the biggest weight in the organization when it comes to impacting employees. A study of 164 CEOs in Fortune 500 companies by A. Forster Higgins & Company[xi] revealed that 95% of them believe their communication influenced employee job performance. The study reported that there was no evidence that communication from CEOs in large companies significantly affects employee behavior. A high-level team leader can make a positive impression by being visible and walking around the company, but this behavior does not make an impact on each employee as a CEO might think. In most companies, it is too difficult for top leaders to know every employee well, so they need to rely on a properly situated, effective management team to do the communicating.

There is a wealth of supporting evidence to show that increasing the position power of managers and frontline supervisors influences employees more and builds organization cohesiveness. In the book *Communicating Change,* T.J. and Sandra Larkin[xii] revealed several research studies showing the importance of empowering managers and supervisors. The more position power a manager or supervisor is perceived to have, the more frontline employees will want to meet and work with that team leader.

Task Two- Review the Five Phases of the Model

There are five phases of the Model. We will discuss these phases on the following pages.

Phase # One-   Pre-Planning- Team Unit Leaders Need to Their Homework

❖ All team unit (division, department and group) leaders need to learn what the corporate growth goals and objectives are going to be for the coming year.

❖ Team unit leaders need to know which direct reports are going to be on the team and something about them. Mulligan & Associates has 15 assessment surveys to help team unit leaders learn about their direct reports. The following are factors to consider when building your team:
  - purpose or mission of the group
  - expertise of the members
  - homogenous vs. heterogeneous grouping
  - group cohesiveness (personalities)
  - tasks or projects to complete
  - size of the group

❖ Team unit leaders need to know how their direct reports perceive the company overall and to identify the weaknesses in the organization that need to be improved.

❖ Team unit leaders need to build team cohesiveness and develop all employees into a performance facilitator and a team mate who brings out the best in others. This can be done through the *Team Engagement Achievement Motivation* Program and *Helping & Performance Facilitator Communication Training Model*

❖ Team unit leaders should assess themselves and direct reports and discuss the results. Then there will be a base to start from in developing champion and championship building (best in our field) objectives.

❖ Team unit leaders need to develop a *cause/ mission statement that* says *"We will become and be the best in our work field/industry"*. Team unit leaders must come up with a phrase that will challenge, excite, motivate, unify and get all employees moving in the same direction- a cause that will bring out the potential in employees and make the company number one and profitable.

❖ Consider the **assumptions** or **anticipated changes** that could impact the business:
  - **Government** – new legislation or laws passed.
  - **Competition** – sales and marketing strategies, pricing, mergers, old and new products, balance of trade, etc.
  - **Economics** – inflation, interest rates, value of the dollar, etc.
  - **Social** - leisure time, buying habits, demographic factors, customer attitudes
  - **Workforce** - availability of skilled workers to stay ahead of competitors, plus how to recruit, develop and retain the best

Phase Two- A Performance Evaluation Committee must be established to monitor and measure the progress of the team unit, team members and team unit leader.

This group must be seen as non partial and one that would give the program credibility. Scores would be reported monthly on team units and individuals and four quarterly assessments reports would be completed to determine where team units and individuals are at that time and what they have to do to be successful by the end of the year. This committee or outside group would present the results and awards at the end of the year.

Phase Three- You will *focus first on the bottom or support side of the triangle-the Team Unit Leader's Plan-*

Unit leaders need to assess themselves and develop and meet personal "best in our field" objectives for themselves. You, the unit leader, should use the assessment results from *Step Four* to develop personal growth objectives. You can then develop your leadership and management skills so you will be more effective in helping your direct reports meet their predetermined growth objectives as well as the unit's championship/profitable objectives.

Phase Three- You will *focus on the left side of the triangle- The Team Unit Plan*.

You will conduct research on your competition and ask your direct reports, customers and other stakeholders to evaluate your organization and unit. You will review the past performance of your organization and unit (division or department). Lastly, you will learn the vision and mission statement of your company or organization and it's future growth goals and objectives. Then you can write champion building goals and objectives for your unit that tie into the organization's plan.

Phase Four- *You will focus lastly on the right side of the triangle-The Team Members' Plans*.

You as the team unit leader should meet with each direct report One-On-One and review the vision and mission statements and "best in our field" objectives for the corporation and your unit (division department or group). You want your direct reports to endorse the objectives plus suggest additional "best in our field" objectives.

You will also put your direct reports through assessment and add personal growth" objectives to the list. You need to identify the tasks with each direct report needs to complete to meet specific objectives The *Task Empowerment Process* explained in *Step Three* can be used to help each direct report become an expert in executing all the tasks assigned to him or her

Task Three- Review What Motivates Employees and How the Model has Built in a Specific Motivator to Inspire Employees

Creating the Right Cause to Inspire Employees

The Model recommends that CEO's and their team unit leaders create a cause (mission statement) that will motivate all employees. This Model recommends to department heads, division heads and corporate team leaders that they must *challenge* their people to become the "best in their field"- champions/expert leaders. The spotlight would be placed on individuals and team units as they work hard to achieve the champion building objectives. Those involved in the program would be applauded as they move forward to meet the champion building objectives so they, their department, division and company can be rated champions. The motivator is challenge. The cause is *Becoming the Best in Our Field* which challenges all employees to set the performance bar high and be able to get over it.

If the leadership of an organization doesn't establish a vision and mission statement, and "best in our field" objectives that will rally everyone together to give 100% effort, the company will never be the best. The company will continue to operate behind it's competition and do work that seems like drudgery to the workers.

Because there is so much self-centeredness and lack of loyalty in the workplace today, it is crucial that a company create a cause that will excite, reward and unify everyone. Anytime you have a cause that each person believes in, you will see people banding together to work hard for that cause. The American Revolution, World War I and World War II were fought in the name of freedom. Everyone believed in the cause and many gave their lives for it. George Bush used the tragedy of 9/11 and weapons of mass destruction (fear) to rally everyone around his decision to invade Afganistan and Irag.

The cause "becoming the best in our field" can be observed each fall as hundreds of college teams join in the pursuit of a national football championship. Everyone associated with the college becomes emotionally involved with the team as it strives to be ranked #1. As the season progresses and the team continues to win advancing in the ranks, the enthusiasm and excitement grows. At the end of the season, the two teams ranked the highest by the College Bowl Series Committee will play against one another for the national championship. This next year the four top ranked football teams will have a play off. To be a national or world champion is quite an honor and will help each college recruit the best high school players in the nation to keep them ranked at the top.

Being a championship organization can be an extremely moving experience. For a period of time, you can call yourself the best of the best. Have you ever played and been part of a championship team? How did you feel about it at that time and afterwards? Was it an experience you will always remember?

The Triangle Team Leadership Model: Becoming the Best in Our Field encourages companies to establish exactly the same atmosphere that colleges create during football season and that is **Becoming the Best in Our Field**

The goal is to help each employee become the best of the best in his/her career field (a champion performer) and then work toward transforming the departments, divisions and company into championship organizations (the best in their particular field).

Companies usually don't play football against other companies, but they do compete against each other for the top spot. Everyone in the organization can work together to establish champion building objectives, that if achieved, would take the company to championship status in the eyes of customers, stakeholders, competitors and stock analysts. If the objectives are growth producing and include meeting the expectations of all stakeholders, everyone will benefit.

The *Performance Evaluation Committee* can operate like opposing coaches and sportswriters (AP and UPI polls) who rate the top 25 college football teams at the end of the year. They can rate the corporation as well as the divisions, departments, and individuals. A plan can be developed and a monitoring system established to keep score as the year progresses. Awards can be given out at the end of the year based on the results.

The concept of being the "best in your field" can create an exciting, motivating and growth-oriented work environment. The motivator "being the best in your field" is illustrated in Maslow and Herzberg's work on the following pages.

What Motivates People
Maslow's Self Actualization Theory

Individuals want to identify their potential and use it to grow. Most individuals use 15% of their potential. Maslow says companies must help employees meet their survival, security and belonging needs first if they are going to become and be the best in their field.

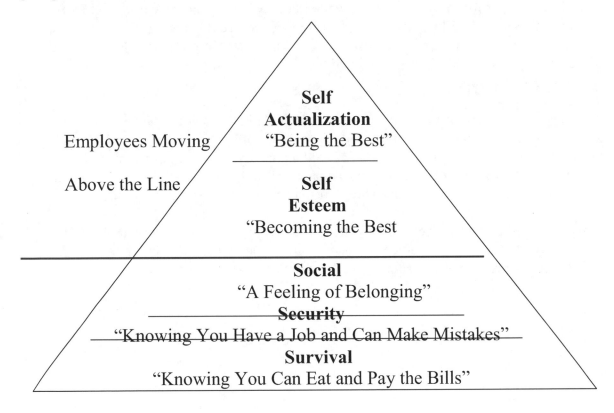

Dr. Maslow's theory states: *if you can meet your survival, security and social needs, you can become and be what you ought to be, the best at what you do.*

Frederick Herzberg's Motivational Model

What Satisfies Employees
Fair company policies and procedures
Effective supervision
Positive relationships with supervisors
Excellent working conditions
Competitive salaries
Productive relationships with peers
Balance between personal life and work
Excellent relationships with direct reports
Status
Security

What Motivates Employees
Challenge
Achievement
Recognition
Responsibility
Advancement
Growth
Additional Compensation

The *Triangle Team Leadership Mode: Becoming the Best in Our Field* focuses more on what motivates employees rather than what satisfies them. *Challenge* is the number one motivator in the *Model* but achievement, giving recognition and responsibility and providing a chance to advance, grow and make additional compensation is also built in the *Model*.

All employees should realize the importance working for a unit or a company that is perceived as the best in their industry. The more recognition an organization receives as being the best, the more other companies will want to recruit employees away. Many leaders working for an outstanding company have been recruited away. The challenge for a company is to make it difficult for talented people to want to leave.

47

Task Four- Learn and Use the _Team Engagement Achievement Motivation_ Program to Launch the Model with Direct Reports

We recommend all team members go through the _Team Engagement Achievement Motivation_ Program together to start The _Performance Triangle Leadership Model._ The _Team Engagement Achievement Motivation_ Program is built on some of the concepts developed by the _Motivation Advancement Program_ of W. Clement and Jesse V. Stone Foundation.   Two concepts of the program are as follows:

Concept One- A fulfilled and motivated individual:
- has personal characteristics, strengths, and abilities that are uniquely his or hers
- is aware of the many resources within himself/herself
- realizes he/she has a purpose within the world and that a pursuit of that purpose is a vital part of his/her fulfillment.
- has a basic desire to change and grow
- has specific meaningful goals and objectives that give direction to personal change, growth and development.
- is profoundly influenced by his/her present environment , which includes associating with those he/she perceives as being successful.

Concept Two- An individual often learns best in an environment that:
- provides action involvement in the learning process
- permits, when possible, the design of his/her own learning situation based on need and desire, rather than a strict order.
- encourages peer to peer involvement in learning
- encourages constructive change through group involvement
- provides opportunities for success in the present and future without reference to the negative past
- encourages the development of one's capabilities by learning from successes

The Program includes six phases.
- _Sharing_-getting acquainted, building a commonality, exchanging information
- _Successes_-opportunity to identify and analyze one's past and present successes
- _Strengths_- Identifying and focusing on unique strengths and discussing how to put these strengths into action through setting and achieving objectives.
- _Values_- identifying & honoring the values that are important to team members.
- _Creative Life Management_- Being able to manage everyday conflicts and problems we face at work and life in a creative manner..
- _Reinforcing the belief we have the talent and capability to succeed._-Developing activities that reinforce constructive behavior patterns so we will succeed.

After the team unit goes through these six phases, we will discuss the _Performance Triangle Leadership Model_ and identify the growth goals and championship building objectives the team unit needs to achieve to claim they are the best in their work fields.

Step Four
Focus on Bottom/Support Side of the Triangle: The Team Unit Leader Plan
Page - (Complete the Following 12 Tasks)

Task One- **Write Out and Review Your Personal Background, Education and College Experience and Work Leadership Positions.**

Personal Background/Education/Work Leadership Positions

FULL NAME: _____

NICKNAME: _____

BIRTH PLACE AND DATE: _____
PARENT'S – NAMES AND OCCUPATIONS: _____

_____

SIBLINGS – NAMES AND OCCUPATIONS: _____

_____

_____

SPOUSE – NAME AND OCCUPATION: _____
CHILDREN – NAME(S) AND AGE(S): _____

_____

_____

DESCRIBE WHERE YOU GREW UP: _____

YOUR PRESENT CAREER FIELD: _____

YOU PRESENT CAREER POSITION: _____

WHAT ARE THE MAJOR CHALLENGES YOU FACE IN YOUR PRESENT POSITION? _____

_____

_____

_____

_____

WHERE DO YOU WANT TO LIVE AND WORK? _____
COMPENSATION YOU ARE EARNING NOW? _____ WHAT IS THE MINIMUM YOU WOULD ACCEPT IN NEXT JOB?

WHAT DO YOU CONSIDER YOUR MAIN STRENGTHS AND WEAKNESSES IN DOING YOUR PRESENT JOB?
STRENGTHS _____

: _____

WEAKNESSES _____

_____

OUTLINE YOUR EDUCATIONAL AND LEADERSHIP POSITIONS IN SCHOOL

INDICATE HIGHEST DEGREE COMPLETED AND THEN FILL OUT CORRESPONDING CHART:

HIGH SCHOOL:	FR	SOPH	JR	SR
COLLEGE:	FR	SOPH	JR	SR

VOCATIONAL SCHOOL: CERTIFICATION: _____

GRADUATE SCHOOL: DEGREE RECEIVED: _____

	HIGH SCHOOL	COLLEGE	COLLEGE
NAME OF SCHOOL AND LOCATION:			
DATES OF ATTENDANCE:			
APPROXIMATE G.P.A. OR CLASS STANDING:			
COLLEGE MAJOR/MINOR STUDIES			
FAVORITE SUBJECT(S):			
LEADERSHIP OFFICES HELD, HONORS, AWARDS:			
ORGANIZATIONS JOINED OR EXTRA CURRICULAR ACTIVITIES:			

PROFESSIONAL CERTIFICATIONS OBTAINED

_____

_____

REVIEW YOUR CAREER PATH AND LEADERSHIP POSITIONS HELD
PLEASE LIST THE COMPANIES/ORGANIZATIONS THAT HIRED YOU, INDUSTRY, THE DATES YOU WORKED WITH EACH ORGANIZATION AND LEADERSHIP POSITIONS THAT YOU HELD.

#	COMPANIES OR ORGANIZATIONS	INDUSTRY	DATES EMPLOYED	LEADERSHIP POSITIONS/JOBS HELD
1				
2				
3				
4				
5				
6				

WHAT CAREER FIELD OR POSITION(S) HAVE THESE WORK/LEADERSHIP EXPERIENCES PREPARED YOU TO DO NEXT?

_____

_____

Task Two- Assess Your Satisfaction with Your Present Career and Position and Balance of Work and Life

The Route 66 Job Satisfaction Survey-Measures Right Work Situation and Rewards

To help you assess if you are satisfied with your career route today, we would like you to fill out the **Route 66 Job Satisfaction Survey** (if in college, fill it out when working)

Right Work Situation – How Satisfied Are You?
(Answer yes if you are satisfied or no if you are dissatisfied to each of the 10 statements)

1. **The career field or industry that I am presently working in is right for me.**
   _____ yes   _____ no

2. **My boss and I have good chemistry and he/she is an effective mentor..**
   _____ yes   _____ no

3. **The career position I occupy presently is right for me.**
   _____ yes   _____ no

4. **The job description and performance expectations by my boss are right for me.**
   _____ yes   _____ no

5. **The company culture (values, behaviors, beliefs about people) is right for me.**
   _____ yes   _____ no

6. **I fit right in with my team unit (peers, direct reports, boss).**
   _____ yes   _____ no

7. **I like the vision and mission of my company/organization.**
   _____ yes   _____ no

8. **I like the career development/advancement program that my company has in place.** _____ yes   _____ no

9. **I like the way my boss and company includes me in the planning process.**
   _____ yes   _____ no

10. **My company and boss rate and treat me fairly.**
    _____ yes   _____ no

Right Financial, Personal and Professional Rewards-How Satisfied Are You?

(Answer yes if you are satisfied or no if you are dissatisfied to each of the 10 statements)

1. I am happy with my total compensation package.

    _____ yes   _____ no

2. I feel like my security and survival needs are being met.

    _____ yes   _____ no

3. I feel like my social and belonging needs are being met.

    _____ yes   _____ no

4. I feel challenged in my present position.

    _____ yes   _____ no

5. I feel like I am growing in my present position.

    _____ yes   _____ no

6. I feel like I am being recognized and rewarded for my achievements and contributions to the company.

    _____ yes   _____ no

7. I have excellent working conditions and benefits.

    _____ yes   _____ no

8. I feel my department and company are striving to be the best at what they do and they want me to be the best at what I do. They provide me with opportunities to grow professionally.

    _____ yes   _____ no

9. I have a balance of work, family and personal life.

    _____ yes   _____ no

10. The company cares about their employees and they show it.

    _____ yes   _____ no

What is Your Job Satisfaction Score?

Right Work Situation   _____

   (add up your yes answers and put the number above)

Right Rewards   _____

   (add up your yes answers and put the number above)

What Route are You on Today? _____/_____

                              Right Fit Number   **Right Rewards**

Number

Are you on route 66 or higher? If not, you need to develop a plan to put yourself on a satisfying career route. Raise your <u>right work situation</u> and <u>right rewards</u> scores to 66 or higher. You want answer yes to six or more questions on the survey.

The pressure to produce (profit) has caused employees to work longer hours, experience more stress and have fewer hours to be with family, friends and do what they want. On a scale of 1 to 10, 10 being <u>extremely satisfied</u> and 1 being <u>extremely dissatisfied</u>, how do you rate yourself in the following areas:

1. **Balancing your work, family and personal life** _____

2. **Managing stress at work and in your life** _____

3. **Staying in top physical condition** _____

4. **Relating with spouse** _____

5. **Relating with children** _____

6. **Relationship with parents and siblings** _____

7. **Relationship with friends** _____

8. **Relationship with boss** _____

9. **Relationship with colleagues** _____

10. **Relationship with direct reports** _____

11. **Relationship with customers** _____

12. **Meeting boss expectations** _____

13. **Meeting your expectations** _____

14. **Where you are in your career** _____

15. **Where you are in your life** _____

Total Score _____

0-50 Terrible   *51-100 Doing Ok*   *101-150 Excellent*

Following are methods used to manage stress. Please check the methods you use.

_____	**Meditation**	_____	**Team support system**
_____	**Massage**	_____	**One-on-one coaching**
_____	**Physical exercise**	_____	**Outside interests**

Other: Explain

A Meaningful Quote

"Before you are a leader, success is all about growing yourself. When you become a leader, success is all about growing others".

Jack Welch
Former General Electric CEO

<u>Task Three</u>-Participate in a 360 degree *Strategic Leadership Development* Program

The Management Research Group in Portland Maine [ix] has developed a 360 degree leadership evaluation program to help organizations develop the strategic leadership practices that team unit leaders should execute. The program asks the organization leaders to identify the six to eight leadership practices, if emulated, would take the organization forward. Then a 360 degree survey is passed out to those who work with each team unit leader. The results are tallied and interpreted to each leader. Each team unit leader is asked to develop a development plan to improve his/her leadership practices in the priority areas. The program helps the leaders practice those leadership behaviors that will make them and the company champion performers. The 22 Leadership Practices that are measured in the 360 degree survey are listed and described below.

Using the scale 1 to 10 (1 least like you) to (10 most like you), write in the number that best describes you. Write in the number by the leadership practice that best fits your behavior or performance at this time. The 22 leadership practices are divided into six areas. You can participate in the 360 degree *Strategic Leadership Program* later by taking the *LEA* and learn where you placed yourself and where others place you.

l) *Creating a Vision*

_____**Conservative**- You study problems in light of past practices to ensure predictability , reinforce the status quo and minimize risk.

_____**Innovative**- You feel comfortable in fast-changing environments, being willing to take risks and to consider new and untested approaches.

_____**Technical**- You acquire and maintain in-depth knowledge in your field or areas of focus; using your expertise and special knowledge to study issues in depth and draw conclusions.

_____**Self**- You emphasize the importance of making decisions independently; looking to yourself as the prime vehicle for decision-making.

_____**Strategic**- You take a long range, broad approach to problem solving and decision making through objective analysis, thinking ahead and planning.

2)Developing a Following

_____**Persuasive**- You build commitment by convincing others and winning them over to your point of view.

_____**Outgoing**- You act in an extroverted, friendly and informal manner; showing a capacity to quickly establish free and easy interpersonal relationships.

_____**Excitement**-You operate with a good deal of energy, intensity and emotional expression; having a capacity for keeping others enthusiastic and involved.

_____**Restraint**- You maintain a low-key, understated and quite interpersonal demeanor by working to control your emotional expressions.

3) *Implementing the Vision*

_____**Structuring-** You adopt a systematic and organized approach; preferring to work in a precise, methodical manner; developing and using guidelines and procedures.

_____**Tactical-** You emphasize the production of immediate results by focusing on short-range, hands-on, practical strategies.

_____**Communication-** You state clearly what you want and expect from others; clearly expressing your thoughts and ideas; maintaining a precise and constant flow of information.

_____**Delegation-** You enlist the talents of others to help meet objectives by giving them important activities and sufficient autonomy to exercise their own judgment.

4) *Following Through*

_____**Control-** You Adopt an approach in which you take nothing for granted. You set deadlines for certain actions and are persistent in monitoring the progress of activities to insure that they are completed on schedule.

_____**Feedback-** You let others know in a straightforward manner on how well they have performed and if they have met your needs and expectations.

5) **Achieving Results**

_____**Management Focus-** You seek to exert influence by being in positions of authority-taking charge and leading and directing the efforts of others.

_____**Dominant-** You push vigorously to achieve results through an approach which is forceful, assertive and competitive.

_____**Productive-** You adopt a strong orientation toward achievement; holding high expectations for yourself and others and pushing a high standard.

6) *Team Playing*

_____**Cooperative-** You accommodate the needs and interests of others by helping them achieve their objectives.

_____**Consensual-** You value the ideas and opinions of others and collect their input as part of your decision-making process.

_____**Authority Oriented-** You show loyalty to the organization by respecting the ideas and opinions of people in authority and using them as resources for information, direction and decisions.

_____**Empathic-** You demonstrate an active concerned for people and their needs by forming close supportive relationships with others.

How did you rate yourself? How many leadership practices did you rate yourself 7 or higher? How many leadership practices did you rate yourself 4 or lower? Please contact Dr. Mike Mulligan or someone from the Management Research Group if you want you and your company to participate in this 360 degree Strategic Leadership Development Program.

Task Four-Fill Out the *Leadership & Management Competency Survey*, Score Your Answers and Identify Weaknesses and Strengths

Listed below are 60 statements on being a leader and manager. Read each statement and rate your competency level to perform the stated task. Please rate yourself on all 60 statements from one to six. 6 designates you are at the expert level and 1 means you see yourself as incompetent at this time in performing the stated task. The higher your rating, the less coaching and developmental work you see yourself needing to perform the stated task.

Rating Scale
6. Expert –unconsciously competent at performing this task-can coach others
5. Extremely competent at performing this task- no need for coaching
4. Average at performing this task-could use a little coaching at times
3. Somewhat competent at performing this task – would like some steady coaching
2. Not very competent at performing this task- a need for coaching
1. Definitely not competent at performing this task-a strong need for coaching

Team Unit Leader Tasks-We ask you to rate your competency level on the following 20 team unit leadership tasks.

1. I know where my organization/unit is today, can gain the input of others and develop a vision of what the organization/unit should become in the future.
        6_____ 5 _____4 _____3 _____2 _____1_____

2. I am a strategic thinker and can work with others to develop ongoing strategies to help the organization/unit achieve it's vision and plan.
        6_____ 5 _____4 _____3 _____2 _____1_____

3. I can create a mission statement with other that can excite, unite and reward every employee and other stakeholders in the organization/unit.
        6_____ 5 _____4 _____3 _____2 _____1

4. I can work with my boss to develop objectives that have the appropriate financial metrics and then assemble a talented team of individuals that will buy in and help us achieve our predetermined objectives and turn our vision and plan into a reality.
        6_____ 5 _____4 _._____3 _____2 _____1_____

5. I can follow my boss and those who have authority over me as well as lead and delegate responsibilities to those that report to me.
        6_____ 5 _____4 _____3 _____2 _____1_____

<u>Rating Scale</u>
6. Expert – unconsciously competent at performing this task-can coach others
5. Extremely competent at performing this task- no need for coaching
4. Average at performing this task-could use a little coaching at times
3. Somewhat competent at performing this task – would like some steady coaching
2. Not very competent at performing this task- a need for coaching
1. Definitely not competent at performing this task-a strong need for coaching

6. I know how to build and manage a network of team unit leaders that can execute with direct reports our ongoing strategies and plans to meet our objectives.

6_____ 5 _____ 4 _____ 3 _____ 2 _____ 1 _____

7. I can motivate and inspire people so they have the confidence to overcome any impediments that may prevent them from performing and achieving the established objectives.

6._____ 5 _____ 4 _____ 3 _____ 2 _____ 1 _____

8. I know my industry and our market place so I can anticipate and facilitate the changes that our organization/unit needs to make to be successful.

6_____ 5 _____ 4 _____ 3 _____ 2 _____ 1 _____

9. I can engage with direct reports so they feel comfortable in providing constructive advice to meet the challenges (objectives) we set for ourselves.

6_____ 5 _____ 4 _____ 3 _____ 2 _____ 1 _____

10. I am a situational leader knowing when I have to be an autocratic or a benevolent dictator and when it is important to be a collaborative and participative leader. Our financial situation and how much time we have to pull ourselves out of a difficult situation will determine my leadership style.

6_____ 5 _____ 4 _____ 3 _____ 2 _____ 1 _____

11. I read a lot and keep up with what is going on in our organization/unit and industry so when I talk, people to listen to me, adopt my ideas and follow me

6_____ 5 _____ 4 _____ 3 _____ 2 _____ 1 _____

12. I call people by their appropriate name, show warmth, respect, respond with empathy and try to find something we have in common so I can develop a relationship with them.

6_____ 5 _____ 4 _____ 3 _____ 2 _____ 1 _____

13. I am continually spotting talent in people and encouraging them to use it in their assigned positions and situations. I am always thinking how their talent can be used to help our unit/organization grow.

6_____ 5 _____ 4 _____ 3 _____ 2 _____ 1 _____

6. Expert – unconsciously competent at performing this task-can coach others
5. Extremely competent at performing this task- no need for coaching
4. Average at performing this task-could use a little coaching at times
3 .Somewhat competent at performing this task – would like some steady coaching
2. Not very competent at performing this task- a need for coaching
1. Definitely not competent at performing this task-a strong need for coaching

14. I am a honest, fair and ethical person and live these values everyday.

    6_____5 _____4 _____3 _____2 _____1_____

15. I am genuinely interested in learning about people in the organization as I like individuals to talk about themselves, their passion, family, concerns and ideas.

    6_____5 _____4 _____3 _____2 _____1_____

16. I like to make people feel important and part of the unit/organization. I write congratulatory letters, give compliments to individuals in a group setting, praise people for their effort and achievements and provide meaningful rewards to those that deserve them.

    6_____5 _____4 _____3 _____2 _____1_____

17. I display enthusiasm and a positive attitude at work and hope this behavior by example will spread throughout our unit/organization.

    6_____5 _____4 _____3 _____2 _____1_____

18. When we have team meetings, I am attentive and show respect for people's ideas so they will continue to share what they know. I believe there is "no one as smart as all of us" and encourage everyone to share their views, ideas and knowledge. I encourage team members not to text, talk on the phone or e-mail others when someone in the group is speaking.

    6_____5 _____4 _____3 _____2 _____1_____

19. I know how to build people's confidence.. If I can't say something worthy about a person, I say nothing. You build people by talking about their strengths and not their weaknesses. You work with people in private meetings to coach them on how to use their strengths and remedy their limitations.

    6_____5 _____4 _____3 _____2 _____1_____

20. I show that I care about each person in my organization/unit. I work with direct reports to set objectives, that if met, will advance their career and the organization/unit.

    6_____5 _____4 _____3 _____2 _____1_____

Management Tasks-We ask you to rate your competency level on the following 40 management tasks.

Rating Scale-
6. Expert- unconsciously competent at performing task-can coach others
5. Extremely competent at performing task - no need for coaching
4. Average at performing task-could use a little coaching at times
3. Somewhat competent at performing task-would like some steady coaching
2. Not very competent at performing this task- a need for coaching
1. Definitely not competent at performing task-a strong need for coaching

21. I am experienced and knowledgeable about the steps in the planning process and feel comfortable in developing realistic and achievable plans.

       6_____ 5 _____ 4 _____ 3 _____ 2 _____ 1_____

22. I know how to collect and analyze data and information (competition, changing market place, customer needs and economic factors etc.) so realistic business objectives and plans can be created by me, my boss and direct reports.

       6_____ 5 _____ 4 _____ 3 _____ 2 _____ 1_____

23. I can effectively work with my boss to develop business objectives and then meet with my direct reports One- on- One to review the objectives, solidify them and add others.

       6_____ 5 _____ 4 _____ 3 _____ 2 _____ 1_____

24. I can implement the *Gap Analysis and Closure Model* (a methodology used to grow an organization/unit) or a similar planning model. This model helps you identify where you are today in an area (sales of a certain product for example), where you want to be at the end of the year and the action plans you need to execute to close the gap.

       6_____ 5 _____ 4 _____ 3 _____ 2 _____ 1_____

25. I can write clear objectives and teach others how to write good objectives so everyone knows what we need to achieve and when.

       6_____ 5 _____ 4 _____ 3 _____ 2 _____ 1_____

26. I can forecast realistic projections of the amount of time, money, manpower and other resources it will take for our organization/unit to achieve it's objectives.

       6_____ 5 _____ 4 _____ 3 _____ 2 _____ 1_____

27. I know all the chart of accounts that go into developing a budget, what we can allocate and spend in each account and how to make everyone in the organization/unit stay within their budget so we can meet our profit objective.

       6_____ 5 _____ 4 _____ 3 _____ 2 _____ 1_____

28. I can read and understand a profit and loss statement, balance sheet and other valuable financial reports that are useful in the planning and monitoring the profit making process.

    6_____5 _____4 _____3 _____2_____1_____

29. I can help direct reports/individuals develop objectives that will tie into their organization/unit's objectives.

    6_____5 _____4 _____3 _____2 _____1_____

30. I can monitor our plan and make the appropriate changes to make sure our team unit/organization stays on course to meet the objectives. This includes building incentives into the plan so team members are motivated and rewarded throughout the year.

    6_____5 _____4 _____3 _____2 _____1_____

31. I can project the human resource needs of my organization/unit and establish an organizational structure identifying the positions necessary to meet our objectives.

    6_____5 _____4 _____3 _____2 _____1_____

32. I can write job descriptions for each position identifying the objectives, tasks, experience, knowledge and special skills and personality needed by an individual to be successful.

    6_____5 _____4 _____3 _____2 _____1_____

33. I can assess my present direct reports to determine if they meet the qualifications that were established for their position. I am astute enough to know whether I should spend the time developing a direct report or releasing him or her.

    6_____5 _____4 _____3 _____2 _____1_____

34. I can work with our human resource department to upgrade the talent in specific positions in my organization/unit.

    6_____5 _____4 _____3 _____2 _____1____

35. I am effective at interviewing people for specific positions, checking out their references and using assessment instruments to learn about them before an offer is made.

    6_____5 _____4 _____3 _____2 _____1____

6. *Expert- unconsciously competent at performing task-can coach others*
5. *Extremely competent at performing task - no need for coaching*
4. *Average at performing task-could use a little coaching at times*
3. *Somewhat competent at performing task-would like some steady coaching*
2. *Not very competent at performing this task- a need for coaching*
1. *Definitely not competent at performing task-a strong need for coaching*

36. I am skilled in process design and improvement, projecting manpower needs, rightsizing and making organizational changes.

   6_____ 5 _____ 4 _____ 3 _____ 2 _____ 1_____

37. I have a process that identifies high potential managers and unit leaders.

   6_____ 5 _____ 4 _____ 3 _____ 2 _____ 1_____

38. I have a process that identifies high potential team member or task leaders.

   6_____ 5 _____ 4 _____ 3 _____ 2 _____ 1_____

39.. I can execute a leadership and performance management system (organization effectiveness model) that transforms all direct reports into champion performers and my organization/ unit into a championship/profitable organization.

   6_____ 5 _____ 4 _____ 3 _____ 2 _____ 1_____

40. I possess good time management and organization skills and use the appropriate technology to get more work done than the average team unit leader/manager.

   6_____ 5 _____ 4 _____ 3 _____ 2 _____ 1_____

41. I can operate as an effective One on One Idiosyncratic Manager (knowing an individual so well that you can help him grow and perform at a high level) and bring out the best in each direct report.

   6_____ 5 _____ 4 _____ 3 _____ 2 _____ 1_____

42. I know the assessment instruments/materials to use to learn about my direct reports. (what motivates and de-motivates them, their career interests, skills, values, needs, desire to be a team unit leader or team member leader and career aspiration).

   6_____ 5 _____ 4 _____ 3 _____ 2 _____ 1_____

43. I am very effective at meeting with direct reports One- on-One to gain their support on the team unit objectives that my boss and I want to achieve. I am also skillful at obtaining their ideas on other growth objectives that will make our unit/organization better.

   6_____ 5 _____ 4 _____ 3 _____ 2 _____ 1_____

6. _Expert- unconsciously competent at performing task_-can coach others
5. _Extremely competent at performing task_ - no need for coaching
4. _Average at performing task_-could use a little coaching at times
3. _Somewhat competent at performing task_-would like some steady coaching
2. _Not very competent at performing this task_- a need for coaching
1. _Definitely not competent at performing task_-a strong need for coaching

44. I can work One- on- One with each direct report and teach them the business planning and the Gap Analysis and Closure Model that we will use to develop our plan.

6_____ 5 _____4 _____3 _____2 _____1_____

45. I am effective at sitting down with each of my direct reports One- on- One and helping them develop their growth (champion building) objectives for the year. Each direct report's objectives will tie into achieving the team unit's growth objectives which includes growing direct reports as well as the unit.

6_____ 5 _____4 _____3 _____2 _____1_____

46. I am effective at meeting with my direct reports One- on- One monthly to monitor and track their progress and make adjustments so the personal and the unit's business objectives are met.

6_____ 5 _____4 _____3 _____2 _____1_____

47. I am effective at meeting with my direct reports One-on- One to maintain harmony and good working relationships between team members. If dissonance is occurring between me and a direct report or between two direct reports, we will solve the issue One- on- One and not in a team meeting where it makes problems more difficult to solve.

6_____ 5 _____4 _____3 _____2 _____1_____

48. I can meet with direct reports One-on- One and identify the tasks they must perform to be the best in their field. I will identify each task and help them move from an unwilling and unable state to an expert (able and willing) position.

6_____ 5 _____4 _____3 _____2 _____1_____

49 I can work One- on- One with each direct report and teach them how to manage and take charge of their career journey.

6_____ 5 _____4 _____3 _____2 _____1_____

50. I can work One- on-One with each direct report and help them become an effective team unit and team member leader. I will suggest they take the Mulligan Leadership Personality Profile, review their results and develop a leadership growth plan for both leadership roles.

6_____ 5 _____4 _____3 _____2 _____1_____

Rating Scale-

6. *Expert- unconsciously competent at performing task*-can coach others
5. *Extremely competent at performing task* - no need for coaching
4. *Average at performing task*-could use a little coaching at times
3. *Somewhat competent at performing task*-would like some steady coaching
2. *Not very competent at performing this task*- a need for coaching
1. *Definitely not competent at performing task*-a strong need for coaching

51. I can collaborate with direct reports and decide on the objectives we must meet to transform ourselves into a championship or high performing unit/organization.

     6_____5 _____4 _____3 _____2 _____1_____

52. I know what assessment tools to use to learn about the group dynamics of our unit. This includes a process that will build team cohesiveness and keep the team moving forward to meet it's objectives..

     6_____5 _____4 _____3 _____2 _____1_____

53. I can establish a monthly and quarterly metric/ monitoring system to keep the team members informed on how they and the team unit are doing in achieving their predetermined objectives.

     6_____5 _____4 _____3 _____2 _____1_____

54. I can conduct monthly motivational meetings so every team member keeps their enthusiasm about transforming themselves and the team unit into the best in the field or class.

     6_____5 _____4 _____3 _____2 _____1_____

55.. I can create a think tank environment where direct reports are rewarded for ideas that help the unit/organization become more streamlined, competitive and profitable.

     6._____5 _____4 _____3 _____2 _____1_____

56.. I am familiar with the literature on what satisfies and dissatisfies people at work. I have a work satisfaction survey I use to learn about my direct reports satisfaction with work and use the information to improve the work and team environment.

     6._____5 _____4 _____3 _____2 _____1_____

57. I know how to use the *normative group process* with direct reports to discover what they view as the major impediments to achieving each unit objective. This process is also used to gain their ideas on how to overcome these impediments to achieve each objective.

     6._____5 _____4 _____3 _____2 _____1_____

58. I am very familiar with the theories on Self Actualization. I know a survey I can use that will tell me if the needs of my direct reports are being met. I know if the security, safety and social needs of my direct reports aren't being met, they will not be able to focus on their job and become the best at what we ask them to do.

     6._____5 _____4 _____3 _____2 _____1_____

    66

<u>*Rating Scale-*</u>
6. Expert- unconsciously competent at performing task-can coach others
5. Extremely competent at performing task - no need for coaching
4. Average at performing task-could use a little coaching at times
3. Somewhat competent at performing task-would like some steady coaching
2. Not very competent at performing this task- a need for coaching
1. Definitely not competent at performing task-a strong need for coaching

59. I can create a helping and performance facilitation work environment with all my direct reports by putting them through the *Team Engagement Achievement Motivation* Program and interpersonal communication training program.

      6._____5 _____4 _____3 _____2 _____1_____

60. I can help the team unit develop an ongoing team unit resume of accomplishments so each team member sees what the unit has accomplished each month and for the year. This builds confidence and unity and help team members develop a strong resume. We can then wave our flag in the organization so we are noticed for our fine work.

      6_____5 _____4 _____3 _____2 _____1_____

Calculate Your Scores for 20 Leadership and 40 Management Tasks

Listed below are *two leadership and four management functions*. There are 10 statements on the survey for each of the six functions. Review each statement on the survey and if you scored a 6, place 15 points by the phrase number below; if your scored a 5, place 12 points by the phrase number below; if you scored a 4, place 9 points on the phrase number below; if you scored a 3, place 6 points on the phrase number below; if you scored a 2, place 3 points by the phrase number below and if you scored a 1, place 0 points by the phrase number below. Then add up all the points to learn your total score for that particular function. Place your total score for each function on the following page and learn the level where you perceive yourself functioning at this time.

Two Leadership Functions

Executing Leadership Tasks
(Assess Where You Are Today and Identify Where You Need to be Tomorrow)
1_____ 2_____ 3_____ 4_____ 5_____ 6_____ 7_____ 8_____ 9_____ 10_____
Total Points_____

Executing Tasks to Build Your Personal Power
(You Want People to Like, Believe in and Follow You)
11._____ 12_____ 13_____ 14_____ 15_____ 16_____ 17_____ 18_____ 19_____ 20_____
Total Points_____

Four Management Functions

Executing Tasks to Develop a Vision and Growth Plan for Your Unit/Organization
(Identify Where You Are Today and Create a Vision and Growth Plan that will Take You Where You Want the Organization to be Next Year at this Time)
21._____ 22_____ 23_____ 24_____ 25_____ 26_____ 27_____ 28_____ 29_____ 30_____
Total Points_____

Executing Tasks that Provides You with the Right Organization and Talent to Make Plan
(You need to identify your human resource needs and then find the talent to make Plan)
31_____ 32_____ 33_____ 34_____ 35_____ 36_____ 37_____ 38_____ 39_____ 40_____
Total Points_____

Executing Tasks that Helps You Build an Effective One on One System to Make Plan
(You manage, motivate and monitor people's progress in One on One sessions to make Plan)
41_____ 42_____ 43_____ 44_____ 45_____ 46_____ 47_____ 48_____ 49_____ 50_____
Total Points_____

Executing Tasks that Helps You Build Team Cohesiveness and Team Play to Make Plan
(You bring everyone together as a team and reinforce team play to make Plan)
51_____ 52_____ 53_____ 54_____ 55_____ 56_____ 57_____ 58_____ 59_____ 60_____
Total Points_____

Review Your Leadership and Management Capability Scores and Functioning Levels

We have combined your 60 answers into two leadership and four management areas. Your total points, which should be recorded in the right column below, will place you on one of five levels. The higher your score and level, the more you perceive yourself as capable of performing the 10 tasks under each area.. The lower your score and level, the less likely you see yourself executing the 10 tasks under the leadership or management areas. Keep in mind that this profile represents the perceptions you have of yourself and is not a test. The score range is 0 to 150.

If you fall at level 5 or at Level 4 with a score of 90 and above, you view yourself as capable of handling most of the 10 tasks included in that one area.. If your score is 60 to 90 and fall at a 3 level, you see yourself as average in carrying out the 10 tasks under the function. If you fall at Level 2 or 1 with a score of 60 or less, you view yourself somewhat opposite of the function or area being described. This information can help you develop yourself into a more effective team unit/member leader.

	150	120	90	60	30	0	
Six Areas	**Definitely Like You Scores of 120 to 150**	**Usually Like You Scores of 90 to 119**	**Somewhat Like You Scores of 60 to 89**	**A Little Like You Scores of 30 to 59**	**Not Like You Scores of 0 to 29**		**Scores**
Leadership **Leading Direct Reports**	Level 5	Level 4	Level 3	Level 2	Level 1		
Building My Personal Power with Direct Reports	Level 5	Level 4	Level 3	Level 2	Level 1		
Management **Developing a Plan**	Level 5	Level 4	Level 3	Level 2	Level 1		
Organizing and Hiring Talent	Level 5	Level 4	Level 3	Level 2	Level 1		
One on One Management	Level 5	Level 4	Level 3	Level 2	Level 1		
Building Team Cohesiveness and Team Play to Achieve the Plan	Level 5	Level 4	Level 3	Level 2	Level 1		

Identify Where You Need to Improve

Leadership

Leading Direct Reports
Building My Personal Power with Direct Reports

Management

Developing a Plan
Organizing and Hiring Talent
One on One Management
Building Team Cohesiveness and Team Play to Achieve the Plan

Task Four- Fill Out the *Mulligan Leadership Personality Profile,* **Score Your Answers and Review Your Results**

Read each phrase below and evaluate the degree to which the phrase <u>describes you</u> *when you are in a performance oriented environment. Please answer all 80 items using the following rating system.*

Rating Scale

6. This statement is <u>definitely</u> like me   5. This statement is <u>very much</u> like me

4. This statement is <u>somewhat</u> like me   3. This statement is <u>partially</u> like me

2. This statement is <u>rarely</u> like me   1. This statement is <u>definitely not</u> like me

1)	I have a high want to achieve and be successful.	6	5	4	3	2	1
2)	I don't accept rejection easily.	6	5	4	3	2	1
3)	I can work alone and account for my actions.	6	5	4	3	2	1
4)	I weigh all the options carefully before making decisions.	6	5	4	3	2	1
5)	I take things as they come and don't panic.	6	5	4	3	2	1
6)	I am an approachable person.	6	5	4	3	2	1
7)	I am a strategic thinker-future oriented and look at big picture.	6	5	4	3	2	1
8)	I promote team cohesiveness.	6	5	4	3	2	1
9)	I am a competitive person.	6	5	4	3	2	1
10)	I have a high will to achieve and be successful.	6	5	4	3	2	1
11)	I march to my own drum beat.	6	5	4	3	2	1
12)	I work hard to avoid making mistakes.	6	5	4	3	2	1
13)	I am cool under fire and keep my composure.	6	5	4	3	2	1
14)	I am a good sounding board for others.	6	5	4	3	2	1
15)	I like to brainstorm and improve the way of doing things.	6	5	4	3	2	1
16)	I am a person who genuinely cares about others.	6	5	4	3	2	1
17)	I am an aggressive person.	6	5	4	3	2	1
18)	I am determined to achieve the objectives I set for myself.	6	5	4	3	2	1
19)	I am my own person.	6	5	4	3	2	1
20)	I am organized.	6	5	4	3	2	1
21)	I can control my emotions when under pressure.	6	5	4	3	2	1
22)	I am a good listener always focusing on what is being said.	6	5	4	3	2	1
23)	I am process improvement oriented, making things better.	6	5	4	3	2	1
24)	I encourage the acceptance of individual differences	6	5	4	3	2	1
25)	I have a sense of urgency in getting things done.	6	5	4	3	2	1
26)	I apply myself to the fullest to complete a task.	6	5	4	3	2	1
27)	I stand my ground when I think I am right.	6	5	4	3	2	1
28)	I am very thorough when working on tasks and projects.	6	5	4	3	2	1
29)	I can control my temper.	6	5	4	3	2	1
30)	I help people improve themselves at what they do.	6	5	4	3	2	1
31)	I am recognized as someone who has good ideas.	6	5	4	3	2	1
32)	I promote coordination of effort between people.	6	5	4	3	2	1
33)	I don't like to lose when I am in a competitive situation.	6	5	4	3	2	1
34)	I move fast to take advantage of new opportunities.	6	5	4	3	2	1
35)	I have a mind of my own.	6	5	4	3	2	1
36)	I am detail oriented.	6	5	4	3	2	1
37)	I stay objective when being attacked by others	6	5	4	3	2	1
38)	I am effective at helping and coaching others.	6	5	4	3	2	1
39)	I am creative.	6	5	4	3	2	1
40)	I promote setting boundaries between people.	6	5	4	3	2	1

6. This statement is <u>definitely</u> like me   **5.This statement is <u>very much</u> like me**
4. This statement is <u>somewhat</u> like me   **3. This statement is <u>partially</u> like me**
2. This statement is <u>rarely</u> like me   **1.This statement is <u>definitely not</u> like me**

41) I make things happen. .	6	5	4	3	2	1
42) I strive to be the best at what I do.	6	5	4	3	2	1
43) I can fend for myself.	6	5	4	3	2	1
44) I am sharp as a tack as nothing gets past me.	6	5	4	3	2	1
45) I am even temperament and steady as a rock.	6	5	4	3	2	1
46) I call people by their name & acknowledge their presence.	6	5	4	3	2	1
47) I like to think situations out before taking action	6	5	4	3	2	1
48) I promote team play.	6	5	4	3	2	1
49) I set high standards for myself and others.	6	5	4	3	2	1
50) I am driven.	6	5	4	3	2	1
51) I prefer to do things my way.	6	5	4	3	2	1
52) I leave no stone unturned	6	5	4	3	2	1
53) I am patient and self disciplined.	6	5	4	3	2	1
54) I reward people for doing what they say they will do	6	5	4	3	2	1
55) I am a curious about how things work and operate.	6	5	4	3	2	1
56) I like to work in a collaborative work environment.	6	5	4	3	2	1
57) I like to be in control and charge of a situation.	6	5	4	3	2	1
58) I move quickly to get things done.	6	5	4	3	2	1
59) I am strong minded.	6	5	4	3	2	1
60) I am technically oriented	6	5	4	3	2	1
61) I believe haste can make waste.	6	5	4	3	2	1
62) I confront those who don't walk their talk.	6	5	4	3	2	1
63) I am a critical thinker.	6	5	4	3	2	1
64) I use positive reinforcement to motivate team mates.	6	5	4	3	2	1
65) I possess an entrepreneurial spirit.	6	5	4	3	2	1
66) I am persistent and see things through to the end.	6	5	4	3	2	1
67) I am a self starter.	6	5	4	3	2	1
68) I am good at gathering facts and investigating situations.	6	5	4	3	2	1
69) I am calm and steady when placed in a negotiating situation.	6	5	4	3	2	1
70) I am effective at bringing out the best in people.	6	5	4	3	2	1
71) I am good at solving problems.	6	5	4	3	2	1
72) I promote team play.	6	5	4	3	2	1
73) I push myself and others to the limit.	6	5	4	3	2	1
74) I am an intense person who likes to be the best	6	5	4	3	2	1
75) I am independent.	6	5	4	3	2	1
76) I am a good researcher and investigator.	6	5	4	3	2	1
77) I am exceptionally poised during heated discussions.	6	5	4	3	2	1
78) I am empathic and respectful toward others	6	5	4	3	2	1
79) I anticipate changes and prepare myself to manage them	6	5	4	3	2	1
80) I believe that you win when you work together as a team.	6	5	4	3	2	1
	6	5	4	3	2	1

Calculate Your Scores for Each of the Eight Personality Traits

Listed below are eight personality traits. There are 10 phrases on the survey for each trait. Please go back to the survey and review your answer on each statement. If you scored a 6, place 15 points by the statement number below; if your scored a 5, place 12 points by the statement number below; if you scored a 4, place 9 points on the statement number below; if you scored a 3, place 6 points on the statement number below; if you scored a 2, place 3 points on the statement number below and if you scored a 1, place 0 points by the statement number below. Then add up all the points to learn your total score for that particular personality trait. *Your scores will range from 0 to 150.* Write your total score for each trait on the following page and identify the level where you perceive yourself functioning at this time.

Competitiveness/Aggressiveness (High Want to Achieve)
1_____ 9_____ 17_____ 25_____ 33_____ 41_____ 49_____ 57_____ 65_____ 73_____
Total Points_____

Determined/Persistent (High Will to Achieve)
2.____ 10_____ 18_____ 26_____ 34_____ 42_____ 50_____ 58_____ 66_____ 74_____
Total Points_____

Self Directed/Independent (Can Do It Alone)
3.____ 11_____ 19_____ 27_____ 35_____ 43_____ 51_____ 59_____ 67_____ 75_____
Total Points_____

Thorough//Detailed/ Investigative(On Top of Things – Hands-On Practical Thinker)
4_____ 12_____ 20_____ 28_____ 36_____ 44_____ 52_____ 60_____ 68_____ 76_____
Total Points_____

Patient/Self Control (Stay Cool Under Fire)
5_____ 13_____ 21_____ 29_____ 37_____ 45_____ 53_____ 61_____ 69_____ 77_____
Total Points_____

Helper/Performance Facilitator (Help Others Solve Their Own Problem and Grow)
6_____ 14_____ 22_____ 30_____ 38_____ 46_____ 54_____ 62_____ 70_____ 78_____
Total Points_____

Innovative/Creative/Strategic (Always Trying to Improve Your Situation &Organization)
7_____ 15_____ 23_____ 31_____ 39_____ 47_____ 55_____ 63_____ 71_____ 79_____
Total Points_____

Team Builder and Player (Always Pulling the Team Together)
8_____ 16_____ 24_____ 32_____ 40_____ 48_____ 56_____ 64_____ 72_____ 80_____
Total Points_____

Your Scores and Functioning Level on Eight Personality Traits

We have combined your eighty answers into eight personality traits. Your total points should be placed in the right column below. Based on your total score, you will fall into one of five levels. The higher your total points and level, the more you are like the trait. The lower your total points and level, the less likely you resemble the trait. The score range is 0 to 150. Keep in mind that this profile represents the perceptions you have of yourself and is not a test of right and wrong answers.

	150	120	90	60	30	0	
Eight Personality Measures	Definitely Like You	Usually Like You	Somewhat Like You	A Little Like You	Not Like You		Scores
Competitive- A High Want to Achieve and be # 1	Level 5	Level 4	Level 3	Level 2	Level 1		
Determined- A High Will to Achieve and be # 1	Level 5	Level 4	Level 3	Level 2	Level 1		
Self-Directed/ Independent	Level 5	Level 4	Level 3	Level 2	Level 1		
Organized/ Detailed Technical	Level 5	Level 4	Level 3	Level 2	Level 1		
Patient/Self Controlled	Level 5	Level 4	Level 3	Level 2	Level 1		
Helpful/ Performance Facilitator	Level 5	Level 4	Level 3	Level 2	Level 1		
Innovative/ Creative Strategic (See Big Picture)	Level 5	Level 4	Level 3	Level 2	Level 1		
Team Builder/ Player	Level 5	Level 4	Level 3	Level 2	Level 1		
	150	120	90	60	30	0	

If you fall at level 5 or at Level 4 with a score of 90 and above, your behavior is more like the trait being described. A Level 3 places you in the average range of likeness. If you fall at Level 1 or 2 with a score of 60 or less, you view yourself somewhat opposite of the trait being described. Once you see where you placed yourself, you need to ask yourself- do I need to be more or less competitive, determined, independent, thorough, patient, helpful, innovative, and a team player to do my job. If so, how do I change my behavior? The scores are reviewed on the next pages.

Interpretation of Eight Trait Scores
Competitive /Aggressive Trait -A High Want to be Number One ©

Personality Measure	Definitely Like You	Usually Like You	Somewhat Like You	A Little Like You	Not Like You	Score
Competitive- A high want to succeed.	Level 5	Level 4	Level 3	Level 2	Level 1	

Range   ←   150   ←   120   ←   90   ←   60   ←   30   ←   0

The higher your score and level, the more:

- You have a high want to succeed and be # one.
- You want to determine the vision, the strategies and the growth objectives of the unit/organization.
- You want to align the organization and select the people who will execute the growth plan.
- You are driven, competitive, aggressive and entrepreneurial.
- You would like to determine the services and products to sell and the customer base.
- You would establish a high standard for yourself and those who report to you and expect everyone to meet the standards that are in place.
- You are motivated by challenge.
- You like to be in control.
- You would like to help establish policies, procedures, structure for everyone to follow.
- You are likely to withstand higher levels of self-imposed pressure and longer duration of stress.
- You would criticize yourself and others when the performance is not at the level you set.
- You might be argumentative, irritable and abrasive with others when things aren't going right.
- You would drive the team forward and meet the organization's vision and objectives.
- Your competitive spirit will generate energy in others.
- You would work hard to convince others to buy your product/service or ideas.
- You would prospect to find customers and money to support the unit/organization.

The Unit Leader/Manager-The competitive/aggressive trait is extremely important in being a unit leader and manager. You have to set performance objectives with direct reports, that if met, will help your organization grow, be competitive and profitable and make your unit the best in it's functional area. A unit leader and manager has to put the performance bar high enough to move the company forward.

Team members are asked to fill a leadership role that requires them to master and execute specific tasks. In essence, team members are asked to step us as expert leaders in a special work area that will help the unit/organization be successful. They have to be competitive, set their own performance objectives and meet them. They need to push themselves.

Self Managers and Sales People- Being *competitive* and setting challenging objectives is a key trait in being a self manager and a successful sales person. In sales, it represents your attitude in going after the business. You must have the want to succeed.

DETERMINED/PERSISTENT TRAIT© *A High Will to be Number One*

Personality Measure	Definitely Like You	Usually Like You	Somewhat Like You	A Little Like You	Not Like You	Score
Determined- A high will to succeed.	Level 5	Level 4	Level 3	Level 2	Level 1	

Range	150	120	90	60	30	0
	←	←	←	←	←	←

The higher your score and level, the more:

- You have a <u>high will to succeed</u> and be # one.
- You are persistent.
- You are determined and hard driving.
- You have a sense of urgency to achieve a task.
- You are eager and active in pursuing the completion of your task.
- You are focused.
- You would raise the energy and the intensity level of those around you.
- You would continuously pursue meeting an objective.
- You want to take the organization and people to greater heights.
- You would be an excellent closer when trying to sell something to a customer or an idea to a fellow employee during a meeting.
- Your boss and team mates/colleagues can depend on you to help them reach the objectives.

Unit Leader/Manger-The *determined/persistent trait* is important in both roles. Unit leaders and managers start out setting achievable and believable objectives with team members. The unit leader and manager needs to develop an environment that motivates all team members to give it their all. If the team unit leader and manager is laid back and does not provide the intensity, determination and energy to raise team members to greater performance heights, the objectives might not be met.

A **Team Member** can raise the intensity level and performance of the team. Michael Jordan of the Chicago Bulls would not allow his team to quit when they got behind in a game. He talked to them, asked them to step it up another notch and willed the team to victory. Each team member must look at how determined, persistent and focused they are on achieving their own objectives as well as the team unit's objectives and then step it up a notch or two. The determination to win or be the best in one's field will help team unit's overcome a lack of talent and rise higher than one could ever expect.

Self Managers and Sales People- Being *determined* is an important trait when trying to achieve your objectives .If you need someone to push you all the time, you might not accomplish as much as you want in life. You probably want to work in a highly structured situation where you are told what to do. In sales where you face a lot of rejection, you need to keep coming back to close the deal. Someone who gives up early would not like a competitive sales territory.

INDEPENDENT / SELF DIRECTED TRAIT© Prefer to Manage Oneself

Personality Measure	Definitely Like You	Usually Like You	Somewhat Like You	A Little Like You	Not Like You	Score
Independent/ Self-Directed	Level 5	Level 4	Level 3	Level 2	Level 1	

Range   150   120   90   60   30   0

The higher your score and level, the more:

- You like to work alone without supervision.
- You want authority and a wide range of freedom to develop and achieve your plan
- You would want the freedom to run your own show and be in charge of your own destiny.
- You are strong minded and firm in the way you do things.
- You are independent and self directed and would like working in an isolated role.
- You would have problems with an autocratic leader/domineering boss.
- You want to develop your own procedures and methods of doing business.
- You like planning, organizing and establishing your own day to day structure.
- You would be difficult to manage.
- You might have difficulty operating as a team player.
- You would have difficulty in following and being controlled by your boss.
- You would want to know the expectations of your boss.
- You would view yourself as a self- starter and self manager and not want much coaching
- You would want to develop your direct reports into or hire self managers.
- You could operate on your own to sell products and services or run your unit

The Unit Leader/Manger-the *self directed/independent trait* is important in both leadership roles. If you are working in the unit leadership/manager role, you need to operate as a self manager. Individuals who work in senior management would be lucky to have a boss who operates as a one-on-one idiosyncratic manager. Normally senior executives are expected to run their own show and report their results daily. Senior executives rise to the top because they can operate independently. The problem is that when senior executives become to independent, they don't know when and what they need to communicate to their boss. They also forget they are a member of the senior executive team and they follow their boss. The goal of all management is to become self directed and transform direct reports into self mangers but keep communication flowing.

The **Team Member** leader needs to work on mastering his/her assigned tasks and meeting the objectives he/she and the boss set when the year first started. The team member needs to work on becoming a self manager. This can be done when the boss uses the *Task Empowerment Process* to help direct reports master their assigned tasks and then be given the authority to work alone.

Self Managers and Sales People- Being *self directed* or operating independently is a must for the sales person who is given a territory and asked to increase sales. He/she must set up appointments with new potential and old customers and get the orders.

DETAILED/THOROUGH/TECHNICAL TRAIT© *Nothing Gets Past Me*

Personality Measure	Definitely Like You	Usually Like You	Somewhat Like You	A Little Like You	Not Like You	Score
Detailed/ Through/ Technical	Level 5	Level 4	Level 3	Level 2	Level 1	

Range 150   120   90   60   30   0

The higher your score and level, the more:

- Your orientation would be toward detail, technical, factual, analytical and investigative work.
- You would enjoy solving intellectual challenges by investigating the facts and concepts associated with a problem or situation.
- You would take a cautious position toward making decisions. This behavior can help colleagues examine their ideas more thoroughly before they make costly decisions.
- You might behave as an intellectual warrior and debate fellow employees so hard and long in a meeting that they might not want to meet with you again.
- You should use your technical orientation to good use.
- You would set up policies and procedures so people know how to operate in the organization.
- You would enjoy doing research and gathering facts to help the organization make decisions.
- You would make sure the organization was compliant with government and banking regulations and other pertinent rules set by the organization.
- You would find unnecessary expenses and keep the unit/organization under budget.
- Your boss would have confidence in assigning you tasks and listening to what you have to say.
- You would operate as a tactical/operation specialist which requires day to day planning.

The Unit Leader/Manager-*Thoroughness, detail and investigative* work is important to senior leaders as well as managers as they develop short and long range strategy.-looking at the big picture of what we need to become and be. If you are working in the unit leadership/manager role, you want to make sure you have done your homework when you hire people, set objectives and tasks and move forward to execute your plan.

Unit/manager leaders need to be more into detail knowing the processes, procedures and policies set by the organization. This includes knowing the process and procedure to follow when recruiting, developing, promoting or releasing employees. Organizations can spend too much money on severance packages and litigation if unit leaders don't follow the rules. Senior unit leaders need to be more thorough when purchasing another company to expand market share. Many organizations have been hurt financially or gone out of business because they paid too much.

Team Members need to be detailed and thorough in mastering their assigned tasks so the organization can be successful. Organizations depend on team member leaders to handle much of the detail and investigative work so the senior unit leaders can develop plans.

Self Managers and Sales People- *Thoroughness* is a must when operating as a self manager and sales person. In sales, you have to make sure you get everything right or you could lose a customer.

PATIENT/SELF CONTROL © NEVER LOSE MY COOL

Personality Measure	Definitely Like You	Usually Like You	Somewhat Like You	A Little Like You	Not Like You	Score
Patient/Self Control	Level 5	Level 4	Level 3	Level 2	Level 1	

Range   150   120   90   60   30   0

The higher score and level, the more:

- You would reflect a calm, steady, unhurried, relaxed, stable and patient manner.
- You can tolerate tasks that require longer periods of time to complete.
- You would take the time to learn about a person and thus be an effective helper/ manager.
- You would spend time transforming a direct report/colleague into a champion performer.
- You would listen to people for longer periods of time helping them explore and understand their situation before developing appropriate action steps.
- You would be viewed as approachable when one needs to talk about a problem.
- You would keep your composure during intense discussions and not make hasty decisions.
- You would take things slowly and would not push the panic button.
- You would be mentally disciplined.
- You would be patient with customers and fellow workers.
- You would wait to push yourself and others into action when the need arises.

The Unit Leader/Manager- *the Patient/Self Control trait* is important in both leadership roles. If you are working in the unit leadership/ manager's role, you want to make sure you are patient and in self control at all times. When an executive becomes angry and frustrated, the/she can make bad decisions and they can come back to hurt you and the unit/organization. There have been stories about CEOs throwing pencils and swearing at their senior management staff as well as firing them on the spot because the sales numbers were not good.

Unit leaders/managers need to work on their One on One Management skills and take the time to help direct reports /team members become expert leaders in their field. This takes *patience* and being in *self control*. As you rise in the management ranks, you don't expect to do as much coaching or be coached because you should already be an expert leader in your field and a self manager. However, you do need to be in control of your emotions.

Team Member Leaders need to be patient and in self control when their bosses and colleagues do and say stupid things. A study by Career Builder recently reported 30 % of the workers said they work for a bully. Team members also need to be patient and in self control when working directly with an obnoxious customer or colleague. Employees who are helpful, patient and in self control with customers and fellow employees are a real asset to an organization.

Self Managers and Sales People- Self managers need to be patient with themselves and sales people need to be patient with customers and underwriters at the home office who could nix a deal.

HELPER/PERFORMANCE FACILITATOR © BRING OUT THE BEST IN OTHERS

Personality Measure	Definitely Like You	Usually Like You	Somewhat Like You	A Little Like You	Not Like You	Score
Performance Facilitator and Helper	Level 5	Level 4	Level 3	Level 2	Level 1	

Range	150	120	90	60	30	0

The higher your score and level, the more:

- You would be someone a person would seek out to discuss and solve a problem/ issue.
- You would be perceived as a person who is caring and a good sounding board.
- You would help someone explore, understand and solve their situation without giving premature advice that could be harmful.
- You would have the capability to respond with empathy to a person who is in an unpleasant emotional state and move them to a logical state so they can think clearly.
- You would help people establish, execute and meet growth objectives.
- You would be described as supportive and accepting of others.
- You would enjoy being in a position to take care of the behind the scenes work and keep the team on course to meet the objectives.
- You would enjoy managing and coaching people so they become an expert leader.
- You would like servicing customers and helping fellow colleagues in the organization.
- You would want to build a helping and performance facilitating work environment.
- You would spot talent in people and help them develop it.
- You would help people move toward their ultimate career position.
- You would build systems to identify talented people and grow them so the organization stays competitive and successful in the years ahead.
- You would confront someone if they are not walking their talk.
- You would challenge individuals to become the best they can be.
- You would set up and execute a leadership and performance management system in your unit/organization to help team members become champion/expert performers and the unit a championship organization.

The Unit Leader/Manager-the *Helper/Performance Facilitator trait* is important in both leadership roles. Everyone in an organization should go through a helping and performance facilitation training program. It is important for employees to learn how to build working relationships with each other, be able to focus listen and target respond when colleagues are talking so in-depth understanding occurs and wise plans can be developed.

If **Team Member Leaders** build working relationships with fellow employees and help each other execute a well conceived plan, the team unit/organization will have a better chance of being successful. All employees should read Dr. Mulligan's *book Sharpening My One-On-One Performance Facilitation and Helping Communication Skills.*

Self Managers usually make effective competitive sales people because they can work alone without supervision and establish their own work plan.

INNOVATIVE/CREATIVE/STRATEGIC © IMPROVES PROCESSES, PRODUCTS AND SERVICE

Personality Measure	Definitely Like You	Usually Like You	Somewhat Like You	A Little Like You	Not Like You	Score
Innovative/ Creative/ Strategic	Level 5	Level 4	Level 3	Level 2	Level 1	

Range   150   120   90   60   30   0

The higher your score and level, the more:

- You would operate as a visionary/strategic thinker, one who is always studying the landscape, seeing the big picture and helping the organization become what it should become and be.
- You would like to brainstorm and come up with ideas that can help the unit/organization.
- You would be looking to improve processes in the organization
- You would be a critical thinker, one who can digest, analyze and synthesize information and use the findings to make future plans..
- You would help people and your organization improve the way things are done.
- You would push people to think out of the box and be more innovative.
- You would like have the opportunity to be creative and work with ideas in your daily work.
- You would think things out before taking action.
- You would be curious about how things work.
- You would keep your antenna up to anticipate and make changes that are necessary.
- You would set up a system to keep up with the latest in your field so you can make improvements in your unit/organization.

The Unit Leader/Manager- *the Innovative/Creative/Strategic trait* is important in both leadership roles. If you are working in the unit leadership/manager's role, you want to make sure you work with others to create a vision of what the unit/organization should be like in the future and develop a plan to get there. The competition will continue to think of ways to be the best in the industry so your organization needs to tap it's brain power as well. Unit leadership needs to find the best minds and bring out the thinking of the present employees. Unit leaders also need to continue to think of how each department and the total organization can get better and stay ahead of the competition. Employees hear about continuous improvement but it needs to be practiced. Many employees have great ideas but no one solicits them.

If **Team Member Leaders** are asked to give their input on various topics, unit leaders will hear some creative suggestions. When team unit leaders sit down to manage their direct reports One on One, this is the time to ask each person how they can improve what they are doing and how the unit and organization can be improved. Psychologists say people use about 15% of their potential. This is because many unit leaders look at their employees as grinders rather than asking them how they and the unit/organization can do things faster and better. Unit leaders need to meet with direct reports and conduct "think tanks" to pull new and creative ideas out of them.

Self Managers and Sales People also need to be creative and innovative.

TEAM BUILDER/ PLAYER© NO ONE SMARTER THAN ALL OF US

Personality Measure	Definitely Like You	Usually Like You	Somewhat Like You	A Little Like You	Not Like You	Score
Team Builder/ Player	Level 5	Level 4	Level 3	Level 2	Level 1	

Range ← 150 ← 120 ← 90 ← 60 ← 30 ← 0

The higher your score, and level, the more:

- You would promote the sharing of ideas.
- You would concentrate on building team cohesiveness.
- You would reinforce continuous team play.
- You would create a collaborative and democratic work environment.
- You would want everyone on the planning team and being accountable for the results.
- You would encourage acceptance of differences of opinion and divergent thinking.
- You would promote acceptance of cultural and individual differences.
- You would increase emotional involvement in team objective achievement.
- You would put the spot light on the team and would wave the team flag.
- You would enjoy a close working relationship with your boss and team mates.
- You would review your job tasks with your boss and be sure of what he/she expects.
- You would execute the Triangle Team Leadership Model which will build team cohesiveness and transform the unit and members into leaders.

The Unit Leader/Manager -the *Team Builder/Player trait* is important in both leadership roles. If you are working in the unit leadership/manager's role, you want to make sure you communicate to your direct reports that it is people who play on championship teams that normally get ahead in the world. You can discuss the 1985 Chicago Bears team who won a super bowl. They not only won rings but obtained great jobs after their football days were over and still have good jobs today.

Team Members need to know that if they play together, they and their unit/organization can become the best at what they do. If this happens, their company will want to keep them and other companies will want to recruit them. Senior management likes to keep people who are talented and best in their field.

Another important point is that if you can build a strong working relationship with all the people that work in your unit and help each other and the unit be successful, there will be one person in the group whose career will take off. As that person moves up the management ladder, they will mostly likely take you with them. Your career can rise on the shirt tail of a fellow worker.

Self Manager and Sales People need to be *a team player* because you can't do it alone.
One might want to operate independently but in almost everything we do, we need the help of someone else.

Task Six- Fill out the Group Leadership Behavior Assessment, Score Your Answers and Identify Weaknesses and Strengths

Identify How You Behave in a Group /Team Meeting

Instructions: There are twenty four verbs listed below that describe some of the ways in which people feel and act in group and team meetings.

Write the **six verbs below** that best describe your behavior when you are **leading a group** or being a **team unit leader**.
1._____ 2._____ 3._____ 4._____ 5._____ 6._____

Write the **six verbs below** that best describe your behavior when you are a **team member** participating in a group meeting and not leading the group session.
1._____ 2._____ 3._____ 4._____ 5._____ 6._____

1) Acquiesce	2) Advise	3) Agree
4) Argue	5) Assist	6) Concede
7) Concur	8) Congenial	9) Coordinate
10) Criticize	11) Direct	12) Disapprove
13) Evade	14) Initiate	15) Judge
16) Lead	17) Object	18) Oblige
19) Passive	20) Persuade	21) Relinquish
22) Resist	23) Retreat	24) Withdraw

Review the next page and see where you fell in the four zones. Do you need to change your behavior to be a more effective team unit and team member leader?

Identify Your Team Unit and Team Member Behavior in Groups

In the boxes below, circle the six verbs you marked to describe your behavior when leading a team or group.
In which zone did you land? _____

In the boxes below, put an x through the six verbs you marked to describe your behavior when you are a member of a team or group.
In which zone did you land? _____

	Like To Control (High Dominance)	Let Others Control (Low Dominance)
Warm and Personal (High Sociability)	Advise Coordinate Direct Initiate Lead Persuade *Zone 1*	Acquiesce Agree Assist Oblige Concur Congenial *Zone 2*
Cold and Impersonal (Low Sociability)	Argue Criticize Disapprove Judge Resist Object *Zone 3*	Concede Evade Relinquish Retreat Withdraw Passive *Zone 4*

The zone in which three or more verbs are circled out of the six represent your interpersonal pattern tendencies in a group or on a team.

- Did you fall in the same zone as a team unit and team member leader?

- Should your behavior be different when playing the two leadership roles?

- What did you learn about yourself from this exercise?

Task Seven-Fill out *The Team Leadership Assessment*, Score Your Answers and Identify Your Weaknesses and Strengths.

READ THE FOLLOWING 20 STATEMENTS AND RATE YOUR SELF ON EACH STATEMENT.
Rating Scale-
6.*Always perform this task*
5. *Usually perform this task*
4. *Frequently perform task*
3. *Occasionally perform task*
2. *Seldom perform this task*
1. *Never perform this task-*

1. I offer facts, provide relevant information and give my opinions, ideas and suggestions so the team discussion will take off.

6_____ 5 _____ 4 _____ 3 _____ 2 _____ 1 _____

2. I encourage all members of the group to participate, demonstrate a receptivity and openness to their ideas and recognize them for their contributions.

6_____ 5 _____ 4 _____ 3 _____ 2 _____ 1 _____

3 I ask for facts, information, opinions from team members to help the group discussion move forward so issues are solved and plans made.

6_____ 5 _____ 4 _____ 3 _____ 2 _____ 1 _____

4. I persuade members to analyze constructively their differences of opinion and proposals and come up with the best ideas and plans for the organization.

6_____ 5 _____ 4 _____ 3 _____ 2 _____ 1 _____

5. I set the stage for the meeting, push the group to develop objectives so we know what needs to be accomplished and how and when are we are going to meet the objectives.

6_____ 5 _____ 4 _____ 3 _____ 2 _____ 1 _____

6. I relieve group tension and increase team cohesiveness by being positive, having a sense of humor, proposing fun approaches to group work and taking breaks at the right times.

6_____ 5 _____ 4 _____ 3 _____ 2 _____ 1 _____

7. I give direction to the group by developing steps on how the group will proceed and by having each member focus on the tasks that need to be done to meet the objectives

6_____ 5 _____ 4 _____ 3 _____ 2 _____ 1 _____

8. I help communication among group members by making sure that what each member says is understood by all

6_____ 5 _____ 4 _____ 3 _____ 2 _____ 1 _____

9. I pull together related ideas or suggestions made by group members and restate and summarize the major points made by them.

6_____ 5 _____ 4 _____ 3 _____ 2 _____ 1 _____

10. I share my knowledge about group work, the way members should interact with each other. and when it is appropriate to twitter or talk on cell phones during meetings. I also ask members how they are feeling about the way in which the group is working together.

6_____ 5 _____ 4 _____ 3 _____ 2 _____ 1 _____

6. Always perform this task
5. Usually perform this task
4. Frequently perform task
3. Occasionally perform task
2. Seldom perform this task
1. Never perform this task

11. I like to work in a collaborative way pulling everyone's ideas and suggestions together to create better plans and ways of doing things.

6_____ 5 _____ 4 _____ 3 _____ 2_____ 1_____

12. I am constantly observing the progress of the group and how effective it is working together.

6_____ 5 _____ 4 _____ 3 _____ 2_____ 1_____

13. I can determine the impediments that are slowing the group down in achieving their goals and objectives.

6_____ 5 _____ 4 _____ 3 _____ 2_____ 1_____

14. I continuously inform the group of it's progress so they know where they are in a point in time and how hard and smart they have to work to meet the predetermined objectives.

6_____ 5 _____ 4 _____ 3 _____ 2_____ 1_____

15. I energize the group members by challenging them to produce a higher quality of work.

6_____ 5 _____ 4 _____ 3 _____ 2_____ 1_____

16..I listen to and weigh the ideas of group members and accept their plan when I think it is well thought out and a wise one.

6_____ 5 _____ 4 _____ 3 _____ 2_____ 1_____

17. I evaluate how practical and workable ideas might be, will test a theory in a real situation to see how it might work and create alternative solutions to problems when it is wise to do so.

6_____ 5 _____ 4 _____ 3 _____ 2_____ 1_____

18.. I accept and support the openness of group members and reinforce individuals taking risks as long as their mistake doesn't destroy the organization.

6_____ 5 _____ 4 _____ 3 _____ 2_____ 1_____

19.I continually compare our group's decisions and accomplishments with past group's standards and accomplishments so I know we are learning from the past and making progress.

6_____ 5 _____ 4 _____ 3 _____ 2_____ 1_____

20. I promote the open and civil discussion of disagreements between group members in order to resolve issues, learn and increase team play.

6_____ 5 _____ 4 _____ 3 _____ 2_____ 1_____

Calculate Your Functioning Level on *Task Leadership Behavior*

Please review the 10 *odd numbers* on the survey which measure your *task leadership behavior* when running groups. If you answered a 6 on a statement , write 15 points by that number below, if you scored a 5, write 12 points by the number, if you scored a 4, write 9 points by the number, if you scored 3, write 6 by the number, if you scored 2, write 3 by the number, if you scored 1, write 0 by the number. Your total score will be from 0 to 150. Your Task Leadership Behavior functioning level will be determined by adding up your total 10 scores and learning what your total score turns out to be.

YOUR TASK LEADERSHIP BEHAVIOR
CALCULATING YOUR TASK LEADERSHIP BEHAVIOR FUNCTIONING SCORE

_____ 1. INFORMATION AND OPINION GIVER: OFFERS FACTS, OPINIONS, IDEAS, SUGGESTIONSAND RELEVANT INFORMATION TO HELP GROUP DISCUSSION.

_____ 3. INFORMATION AND OPINION SEEKER: ASKS FOR FACTS, INFORMATION, OPINIONS, IDEAS AND FEELINGS FROM OTHER MEMBERS TO HELP GROUP DISCUSSION AND BUILD TOGETHERNESS.

_____ 5. STARTER: PROPOSES ESTABLISHING OBJECTIVES, ACTION STEPS AND TASKS TO INITIATE ACTION WITHIN THE GROUP.

_____ 7. DIRECTION GIVER: DEVELOPS STEPS ON HOW TO PROCEED AND FOCUSES ATTENTION ON THE STEPS TO BE COMPLETED.

_____ 9. SUMMARIZER: PULLS TOGETHER RELATED IDEAS OR SUGGESTIONS AND RESTATES AND SUMMARIZES MAJOR POINTS DISCUSSED.

_____ 11.COORDINATOR: SHOWS RELATIONSHIPS AMONG VARIOUS IDEAS BY PULLING THEM TOGETHER AND HARMONIZES ACTIVITIES OF VARIOUS SUBGROUPS AND MEMBERS.

_____ 13.DIAGNOSES: FIGURES OUT THE IMPEDIMENTS THAT BLOCK THE TEAM'S PROGRESS- MEETS ONE ON ONE WITH CERTAIN PEOPLE TO REMOVE THE IMPEDIMENTS AND MOVE THEGROUP FORWARD

_____ 15. ENERGIZER: BRINGS OUT ENERGY IN OTHERS AND STIMULATES A HIGHER QUALITY OF WORK FROM THE TEAM.

_____ 17. REALITY TESTER: EXAMINES THE PRACTICALITY AND WORKABILITY OF IDEAS, IDENTIFIES ALTERNATIVE SOLUTIONS AND APPLIES THEM TO REAL SITUATIONS TO SEE IF THEY WORK

_____ 19. EVALUATOR: COMPARES GROUP DECISIONS AND ACCOMPLISHMENTS WITH THE TEAM'S PAST STANDARDS.

_____ TOTAL SCORE - WHAT LEVEL ARE YOU FUNCTIONING? _____

LEVEL 5 *(150 TO 120)* LEVEL 4 (120 TO 90) LEVEL 3 (90 TO 60) LEVEL 2 (60 TO 30) LEVEL 1 (30 TO 0)

Calculate Your Functioning Level on *Maintenance Leadership* Behavior

Please review the 10 *even numbers* on the survey which measure your *maintenance leadership behavior* when running groups. If you answered a 6 on a survey statement, write 15 points by that number below, if you scored a 5, write 12 points by the number, if you scored a 4, write 9 points by the number, if you scored 3, write 6 by the number, if you scored 2, write 3 by the number, if you scored 1, write 0 by the number. Your Maintenance Leadership Behavior level. Your total score will be determined by adding up your total 10 scores on the 10 survey statements and will be from 0 to 150.

YOUR MAINTENANCE/TEAM BUILDING LEADERSHIP BEHAVIOR
CALCULATING YOUR TEAM MAINTENANCE FUNCTIONING SCORE

_____ 2. ENCOURAGER OF PARTICIPATION: WARMLY ENCOURAGES EVERYONE TO PARTICIPATE, GIVING RECOGNITION FOR CONTRIBUTIONS, DEMONSTRATING ACCEPTANCE AND OPENNESS TO IDEAS OF OTHERS.

_____ 4. HARMONIZER AND COMPROMISER: PERSUADES MEMBERS TO ANALYZE CONSTRUCTIVELY THEIR DIFFERENCES OF OPINIONS AND SEARCH FOR COMMON ELEMENTS IN CONFLICTS AND TRY TO RECONCILE THEM.

_____ 6. TENSION RELIEVER: EASES TENSIONS AND INCREASES THE ENJOYMENT OF GROUP MEMBERS BY JOKING, DEMONSTRATING A SENSE OF HUMOR, SUGGESTING BREAKS AND PROPOSING FUN APPROACHES TO GROUP WORK.

_____ 8. COMMUNICATION HELPER: DEMONSTRATES EFFECTIVE COMMUNICATION SKILLS IN HELPING GROUP MEMBERS BETTER UNDERSTANDS SITUATIONS AND CHALLENGES SO BETTER SOLUTIONS CAN BE DEVELOPED AND EXECUTED.

_____ 10. EVALUATOR OF EMOTIONAL CLIMATE: SPOT DISSONACE BETWEEN GROUP MEMBERS AND TRIES TO SOLVE DIFFERENCES IN A SKILLFUL MANNER.

_____ 12. PROCESS OBSERVER: WATCHES THE PROCESS BY WHICH THE GROUP IS WORKING AND MAKES MODIFICATIONS TO FACILITATE BETTER TEAM PLAY.

_____ 14. STANDARD SETTER: DETERMINES GROUP STANDARDS AND OBJECTIVES TO MAKE MEMBERS AWARE OF THE DIRECTION OF THE WORK AND SEEKS ACCEPTANCE OF GROUP NORMS AND PROCEDURES.- ONE EXAMPLE WOULD BE NO TEXTING AND CALLS DURING A MEETING UNLESS RELEVANT TO MEETING.

_____ 16. ACTIVE LISTENER: LISTENS AND SERVES AS AN INTERESTED AUDIENCE FOR OTHER MEMBERS, IS RECEPTIVE TO OTHER IDEAS, GOES ALONG WITH THE TEAM WHEN NOT IN DISAGREEMENT

_____ 18.TRUST BUILDER: ACCEPTS AND SUPPORTS OPENNESS OF OTHER GROUP MEMBERS, REINFORCING RISK TAKING AND ENCOURAGING INDIVIDUALITY.

_____ 20..INTERPERSONAL PROBLEM SOLVER: MEET ONE ON ONE WITH EACH GROUP MEMBER AND DISCUSS THE PROBLEMS THAT THEY MAY BE HAVING WITH SOMEONE IN THE GROUP. DISCUSS HOW YOU WOULD APPRECIATE THE TWO OF THEM WORKING TOGETHERTO CHANGE THE GROUP INTO A TEAM.

_____ TOTAL SCORE- WHAT LEVEL ARE YOU FUNCTIONING? _____

LEVEL 5 (150 TO 120)- LEVEL 4 (120 TO 90) -LEVEL 3 (90 TO 60)- LEVEL 2 (60 TO 30)- LEVEL 1 (30 TO 0)

<u>Task Eight</u>- Fill Out the *Personal Values Assessment Survey,* Score Your Answers and Review Your Results

Below is a list of values and their definitions. Review this list and use the definitions listed to rate your values on the following page. When we occupy a team unit role or team member role, our value system is always at work. If we do not honor or live the values that are most important to us, we need to evaluate what we are doing or not doing and make changes so we can live within ourselves.

1. ACHIEVEMENT - Accomplishment; a result brought about by resolve, persistence, or endeavor. The work "achieve" is defined as "to bring to a successful conclusion; accomplishment or to attain a desired end or aim."

2. ALTRUISM - Regard for or devotion to the interests of others.

3. AUTONOMY - The ability to be a self manager.

4. CREATIVITY - The creating of new and innovative ideas and designs.

5. EMOTIONAL WELL-BEING - Freedom from overwhelming anxieties and barriers to effective functioning; a peace of mind; inner security.

6. HEALTH - The condition of being sound in body; freedom from physical disease or pain; the general condition of the body; well-being.

7. HONESTY - Fairness or straightforwardness of conduct; integrity; uprightness of character or action and authentic (not a pretender)

8. JUSTICE - The quality of being impartial or fair; righteousness; conformity to truth, fact, or reason; to treat others fairly or adequately.

9. KNOWLEDGE - The seeking of truth, information or principles for the satisfaction of curiosity, for use, or for the power of knowing.

10. LOVE - Affection based on admiration or benevolence; warm attachment, enthusiasm, or devotion; unselfish devotion that freely accepts another in loyalty and seeks his good.

11. LOYALTY – Maintaining allegiance to a person, group, institution, or political entity.

12. MORALITY – The belief in and keeping of ethical standards.

13. PHYSICAL APPEARANCE – Concern for the beauty and looks of one's own body.

14. PLEASURE – The agreeable emotion accompanying the possession or expectation of what is good or greatly desired. "Pleasure" stresses satisfaction or gratification rather than visible happiness; a state of gratification.

15. POWER – Possession of control, authority, or influence over others.

16. RECOGNITION – Being made to feel significant and important; being given special notice or attention by others

17. RELIGIOUS FAITH – Obedience to and activity on behalf of a Supreme Being.

18. SKILL – The ability to use one's knowledge, technical expertise and physical attributes effectively and readily in execution of performance;

19. TRUST – Knowing that you have the backing of a person and he/she is on your side.

20. WEALTH – Abundance of valuable material possessions or resources; affluence.

21. WISDOM – The ability to discern inner qualities and relationships; insight, good sense, judgment and make wise decisions

RATE YOUR VALUES

Each of the groups below contains five values. In the parenthesis preceding each value, place a number from 1 to 5. Number 5 represents your HIGHEST ranking value in that group; number 1 represents the value you rank the LOWEST in that group.   Repeat the same process 21 times, total your scores on next page and circle your five highest scores .

1 [   ] Achievement
   [   ] Altruism
   [   ] Justice
   [   ] Religious Faith
   [   ] Wealth

2 [   ] Altruism
   [   ] Autonomy
   [   ] Loyalty
   [   ] Power
   [   ] Recognition

3 [   ] Creativity
   [   ] Love
   [   ] Pleasure
   [   ] Recognition
   [   ] Wealth

4 [   ] Trust
   [   ] Justice
   [   ] Pleasure
   [   ] Power
   [   ] Wisdom

5 [   ] Altruism
   [   ] Honesty
   [   ] Love
   [   ] Physical Appearance
   [   ] Wisdom

6 [   ] Achievement
   [   ] Trust
   [   ] Health
   [   ] Honesty
   [   ] Recognition

7 [   ] Achievement
   [   ] Autonomy
   [   ] Physical Appearance
   [   ] Pleasure
   [   ] Skill

8 [   ] Autonomy
   [   ] Emotional Well Being
   [   ] Health
   [   ] Wealth
   [   ] Wisdom

9 [   ] Honesty
   [   ] Knowledge
   [   ] Power
   [   ] Skill
   [   ] Wealth

10 [   ] Achievement
   [   ] Emotional Well-being
   [   ] Love
   [   ] Morality
   [   ] Power

11 [   ] Trust
   [   ] Autonomy
   [   ] Knowledge
   [   ] Love
   [   ] Religious Faith

12 [   ] Trust
   [   ] Loyalty
   [   ] Morality
   [   ] Physical Appearance
   [   ] Wealth

13 [   ] Creativity
   [   ] Health
   [   ] Physical Appearance
   [   ] Power
   [   ] Religious Faith

14 [   ] Health
   [   ] Justice
   [   ] Love
   [   ] Loyalty
   [   ] Skill

15 [   ] Trust
   [   ] Altruism
   [   ] Creativity
   [   ] Emotional Well-being
   [   ] Skill

16 [   ] Emotional Well-being
   [   ] Justice
   [   ] Knowledge
   [   ] Physical Appearance
   [   ] Recognition   37

17 [   ] Altruism
   [   ] Health
   [   ] Knowledge
   [   ] Morality
   [   ] Pleasure

18 [   ] Morality
   [   ] Recognition
   [   ] Religious Faith
   [   ] Skill
   [   ] Wisdom

19 [   ] Emotional Well-Being
   [   ] Honesty
   [   ] Loyalty
   [   ] Pleasure
   [   ] Religious Faith

20 [   ] Achievement
   [   ] Creativity
   [   ] Knowledge
   [   ] Loyalty
   [   ] Wisdom

21 [   ] Autonomy
   [   ] Creativity
   [   ] Honesty
   [   ] Justice
   [   ]

1. ACHIEVEMENT –
1_____
6_____
7_____
10_____
20_____
Total_____

2. ALTRUISM –
1_____
2_____
5_____
15_____
17_____
Total_____

3. AUTONOMY –
2_____
7_____
8_____
11_____
21_____
Total_____

4. CREATIVITY –
3_____
13_____
15_____
20_____
21_____
Total_____

5. EMOTIONAL WELL-BEING –
8_____
10_____
15_____
16_____
19_____
Total_____

6. HEALTH –
6_____
8_____
13_____
14_____
17_____
Total_____

7. HONESTY -
5_____
6_____
9_____
19_____
21_____
Total_____

8. JUSTICE –
1_____
4_____
14_____
16_____
21_____
Total_____

9. KNOWLEDGE –
9_____
11_____
16_____
17_____
20_____
Total_____

10. LOVE –
3_____
5_____
10_____
11_____
14_____
Total_____

11. LOYALTY –
2_____
12_____
14_____
19_____
20_____
Total_____

12. MORALITY –
10_____
12_____
17_____
18_____
21_____
Total_____

13. PHYSICAL APPEARANCE –
5_____
7_____
12_____
13_____
16_____
Total_____

14. PLEASURE –
3_____
4_____
7_____
17_____
19_____
Total _____ **91**

15. POWER –
2_____
4_____
9_____
10_____
13_____
Total_____

16. RECOGNITION –
2_____
3_____
6_____
16_____
18_____
Total_____

17. RELIGIOUS FAITH
1_____
11_____
13_____
18_____
19_____
Total_____

18. SKILL –
7_____
9_____
14_____
15_____
18_____
Total_____

19. TRUST –
4_____
6_____
11_____
12_____
15_____
Total_____

20. WEALTH –
1_____
3_____
8_____
9_____
12_____
Total_____

21. WISDOM –
4_____
5_____
8_____
18_____
20_____
Total_____

**_Task Nine_-Fill Out_the Emotional Intelligence Assessment Survey,
Score Your Answers and Review Your Results**

**_Team Unit Leaders Need to Operate with a High Emotional Quotient (E.Q.) to be
successful-Please assess yourself to determine your E.Q. today_**

Please rate yourself on the following 30 statements. Evaluate yourself on a
scale of 0 to 6, with 6 representing <u>definitely like you</u> and 0 representing
definitely <u>not like you</u>. Place the number that best represents you.

    __ 1.   I am aware of my interests, skills, experiences, talent, values,
and leadership ability.

    — 2.   I never let things or others upset me so much that I blow up or
lose my cool.

    — 3.   I am aware of what motivates me and de-motivates me.

    — 4.   I am very effective at identifying the feelings of others and
stating their feelings back to that person showing empathy.

    — 5.   I have the ability to listen and influence others.

    — 6.   I am aware of my limitations and know what I need to work
on to develop them into strengths.

    — 7.   I am aware of my obsessions and know when I become overly
compulsive.

    — 8.   I am constantly striving to improve and meet my own
standard of excellence.

    — 9.   I am very sensitive to other people's feelings and I am a
caring person.

    — 10.   I can negotiate and resolve disagreements.

    — 11.   I am aware of my emotions and know what causes me to be in
these different states.

    — 12.   I can establish my own objectives, plan of action and work
structure.

    — 13.   I am committed to pursuing the growth goals and achieving
the objectives of my team, organization and
college/university.

    — 14.   I can help others identify their developmental needs and
bolster their confidence to be the best they can be.

Evaluate yourself on a scale of 0 to 6, with 6 representing <u>definitely like you</u> and 0 representing definitely <u>not like you</u>. Place the number that best represents you.

___15   I have the ability to inspire and lead individuals.

— 16.   I have a strong sense of self worth and know I am capable of being the best I can be.

— 17.   I take responsibility for my own actions and personal performance.

— 18.   I am always ready and alert to act on opportunities that make me, my team and organization better.

— 19.   I can anticipate, recognize and meet the needs of others.

__ 20.   I have the ability to initiate and manage change.

— 21.   I know when I say something that offends others.

— 22.   I am very flexible and adaptable.

— 23.   I am always optimistic and look at the glass as half full instead of half empty.

— 24.   I realize that you can cultivate opportunities and success through people who have different experiences, backgrounds and come from different cultures.

— 25.   I am extremely effective at creating group synergy and pursuing collective goals.

— 26.   I know what career positions would be best for me at this time in my career.

— 27.   I am very comfortable with novel ideas, approaches and new information that changes situations.

— 28.   I have a high want and high will to win.

— 29.   I am politically astute, being able to read the group's emotional currents and power relationships.

— 30.   I am extremely effective at creating group synergy and pursuing collective goals.

Please place your answers on the following pages to determine your Emotional Intelligence (E.Q.) score.

Determining Your E.Q. Score

.Dr. Goleman breaks emotional intelligence into five competencies. Three competencies are categorized under *Personal Competence* and the other two are placed under *Social Competence.*

Personal Competence
(Three categories)
1.   *Self Awareness*
- Emotional awareness
- Accurate self assessment
- Self confidence

Write below the numbers or answers you placed for each of the six statements.

1. _____ 6. _____ 11. _____ 16. _____ 21. _____ 26. _____

Total Score: _____ (Add up your six scores above)

2.   *Self Regulation*
- Self control
- Trustworthiness
- Conscientiousness
- Adaptability
- Innovation

Write below the numbers or answers you placed for each of the six statements.

2. _____ 7. _____ 12. _____ 17. _____ 22. _____ 27. _____

Total Score: _____ (Add up your six scores above)

3.   *Motivation*
- Achievement driven
- Committed
- Initiative
- Optimistic

Write below the numbers or answers you placed for each of the six statements.

3. _____ 8. _____ 13. _____ 18. _____ 23. _____ 28. _____

Total Score: _____ (Add up your six scores above)

<u>*Social Competence*</u>
(Two categories)
1.   *Empathy*
- **Understanding other people's feelings**
- **Developing others**
- **Service orientation**
- **Leveraging diversity**
- **Political awareness**

Write below the numbers or answers you placed for each of the six statements.
4. _____   9. _____   14. _____   19. _____   24. _____   29. _____

Total Score: _____ (Add up your six scores above)
2.   *Social Skills*
- **Influence**
- **Communication**
- **Conflict management**
- **Leadership**
- **Change catalyst**
- **Building bonds**
- **Collaboration and cooperation**
- **Team capabilities**

Write below the numbers or answers you placed for each of the six statements.
4. _____   10. _____   15. _____   20. _____   25. _____   30. _____

Total Score: _____ (Add up your six scores above)

Self Awareness   _____
Self Regulation   _____
Motivation   _____
Empathy   _____
Social Skills   _____
Five Total Scores   _____ **(Your E. Q. Score)**

<u>**Total Emotional Intelligence Maturity Score**</u>

180-150   **Extremely mature**
149-120   **Above average maturity**
119-90   **Average maturity**
89-60   **Below average in maturity**
59-   **Extremely immature**

Goleman's Research on Emotional Intelligence

Daniel Goleman defines emotional intelligence as "managing feelings so that they are expressed appropriately and effectively, enabling people to work together to accomplish their common goals. Daniel Goleman, in his book: <u>Working with Emotional Intelligence</u>, discussed three areas that make us successful on the job. They are:

- I.Q. – our ability to comprehend and learn things quickly
- Technical expertise and experience
- E.Q.-Emotional intelligence

Goleman discovered that emotional intelligence had to do more with emerging as a leader and becoming a star performer than I.Q. and technical expertise.

David McClelland found that outstanding performers were not just strong in initiative or influence but had strengths across the board, which included the five emotional intelligence areas: *self-awareness, self-regulation, motivation, empathy and social skills.*

McClelland discovered that the emotional competencies that most often led to star status were:

- Initiative, achievement, drive and adaptability
- Influence, team leadership and political awareness
- Empathy, self-confidence and developing others

The two most common traits that prevented people from becoming star performers were:
- Rigidity: These individuals were unable to adapt their style to changes in the organizational culture or to be flexible or to respond to feedback about traits they needed to change or improve. They couldn't listen or learn.

- Poor Relationships: This was the most single frequently mentioned factor. Individuals were being too harshly critical, insensitive or demanding and this alienated those that work for and with that person.

Daniel Goleman conducted research using his competence model with 181 different job positions in 121 companies worldwide. The model asked management to profile excellence for each job. Emotional competence mattered twice as much as I.Q. and expertise. Since 1918, the average I.Q. score in the United States has risen 24 points. Goldman says that as students have grown smarter in I.Q., their emotional intelligence has declined. This means students are growing more lonely, depressed, angry, unruly, nervous, impulsive, aggressive and prone to worry. If this is not corrected, students will be coming to the workplace with lower emotional intelligence, which creates a major challenge for companies in the future.

<u>Task 10</u>-Fill Out the Interpersonal Communication Assessment

Interpersonal Communication Assessment
(Evaluating Yourself as a Helper/Performance Facilitator)

Please answer the following 25 statements using the following scale
  1- Never   2- Seldom   3- Sometimes   4-Usually   5- Always

1. When someone is talking directly to me or to our
    group, my eye contact, facial expressions and
    posture send the message I am interested in what
    that person has to say.   1   2   3   4   5

2. I acknowledge people's presence by saying hello
    and calling them by their appropriate name.   1   2   3   4   5

3. I focus listen so distractions don't get
    in the way of my identifying the feelings and
    messages that a person is sending.   1   2   3   4   5

4. I target respond to help others better
    understand their situation so they can develop their
    ideas, make decisions and solve problems.   1   2   3   4   5

5. When individuals are in an unpleasant mood,
    I respond with empathy, labeling what they
    are feeling so they can work through
    issues, problems and any anger they feel.   1   2   3   4   5

6. My non-verbal and verbal communication
    style reflects my respect for others and shows that
    I believe in their ability to solve their own problems   1   2   3   4   5

7. I work hard developing a trust base and common
    ground between others and myself.   1   2   3   4   5

8. I am careful about taking time away from
    others but know when it is appropriate to do so.   1   2   3   4   5

9. I work closely with my manager/direct report to
    develop and achieve objectives that help my
    department and organization meet their plan.   1   2   3   4   5

1- Never   2- Seldom   3- Sometimes   4-Usually   5- Always

10. I put objectives, plans and status reports into   1   2   3   4   5
    writing and circulate them to keep people
    informed.

11. I work closely with my manager/direct   1   2   3   4   5
    report using a special coaching program
    to progress in becoming an expert in my assigned tasks.

12. I meet with my manager/direct report monthly,   1   2   3   4   5
    One-on-One, to evaluate my/his contribution
    to the department's objectives and discuss how
    I/he can improve and help the team next month.

13. I meet with my manager/direct report a minimum   1   2   3   4   5
    of once a month to discuss the objectives in the
    business plan assessing if all partner expectations
    and the objectives are being met.

14. I attend with my manager and colleagues the   1   2   3   4   5
    team meetings monthly and implement the
    tasks that need to be done to be successful.

15. I work with my manager/direct report to build a   1   2   3   4   5
    career pathing profile so I/he can better direct,
    manage and market my career.

16. I always do what I say I will do. I walk my talk. 1   2   3   4   5

17. I maintain a positive attitude and create   1   2   3   4   5
    excitement, enthusiasm and energy in others.

18. I have a positive attitude during the day and keep 1   2   3   4   5
    a sense of humor to keep things in perspective.

19. I spot talent and strengths in others and   1   2   3   4   5
    encourage them to use it.

1.- Never   2- Seldom   3- Sometimes   4-Usually   5- Always

20. I am a team maker promoting performance   1   2   3   4   5
    facilitating partnerships, and partners helping partners.

21. I communicate with others so everyone knows   1   2   3   4   5
    what is expected, what has been done and what
    needs to be done.

22. I praise, give credit where credit is due and show   1   2   3   4   5
    appreciation to others based on what they accomplish.

23. I provide feedback to others, both positive   1   2   3   4   5
    and negative, in a tactful manner and on a
    continuous basis.

24. I constructively confront others when it is   1   2   3   4   5
    necessary to point out discrepancies so
    everyone is back on the same page.

25. I think before I speak so I don't put others on   1   2   3   4   5
    the defensive. I try to keep myself and others
    in an adult state so we can carry on a logical
    discussion.

TOTAL SCORE _____ MEAN SCORE _____

Did you have a mean score of 4.0 and above?
If not, in what areas do you need to work on at this time?

<u>Task 11</u>-Critique Your Present Performance Management System

Definition of a Performance Management System

A performance management system is a process where you set and achieve objectives. You determine where you are today (in specific growth areas), where you want to be tomorrow (in those same areas) and have a plan to get there (developing and managing a step by step process of tasks to achieve your objectives). There are individual performance management plans and team unit performance management plans. Meeting the team unit objectives depends on how individuals meet their objectives.

The task of developing and implementing a performance management system for yourself is much easier than doing it with a number of direct reports. When you are establishing a performance management system for a team unit, you have to obtain a buy in on the team objectives and then work with and through everyone on the team to achieve the objectives. Your performance and success will depend on a number of factors:

- Having the right people in place and gaining their cooperation and support
- The level of difficulty of the objectives and the time line you have to achieve the objectives.
- Whether you and your staff believe the objectives are achievable.
- The level of authority and position power you have and give to direct reports to achieve the objectives.
- Having the budget and necessary resources to do the job.
- Believing the company has the best products and service in the industry.
- The unknowns in the market place.
- Having an excellent working relationship with your boss, direct reports, and the employees who you need to support you.
- The performance management system you have in place.

A team unit leader has to establish a *performance management system* that helps his/her unit, division and the corporation set and meet growth objectives. This process should increase the value of the company stock, and transform direct reports into expert leaders/ champion performers and the team units, divisions and the company into the best in their fields. A win-win performance management system will give everyone in the company a chance to be rewarded financially as well as grow and advance their career. An effective performance management system will provide team unit leaders with a process they can use through out their career journey to be successful in each team unit position they fill. This system works for nonprofit organizations as well as profit focused groups.

100

Your Present Performance Management System or Process

**Briefly Describe Your Performance Management System and Rate it's Success?
Using the scale 0 to 10 ----0-Poor- 10 Extremely Effective--Your Rating Score _____**

**Briefly Describe How Your Company, Division, and Department
Establish Their Growth Objectives and Work Together.**

Briefly Describe How the Growth Objectives are Monitored.

**Are Your Employees Motivated to Achieve the Growth Objectives of the Company,
Division and Department? If Not, What Steps Should be Taken to Motivate Them?**

. How do You Build Team Cohesiveness?

Briefly Evaluate the Strengths and Weaknesses of Your System.

Task 12-Identify Your Career Aspiration, Next Job Target, Review Your Assessment Results and Develop Growth Objectives

As you plan your career in a rolling five year time line, you might have the same career aspiration for your entire life or your career aspiration can change every three to five years. We listed 15 factors below that can impact the decision making process in developing a career aspiration. They are:

1) The family into which you are born – your parents' expectations of you

2) Your success in school – level of educational achievement

3) Talent awareness through teachers, coaches and parents

4) The education, experience, skills and work knowledge you acquire (capabilities) and vision of what you can do in the world of work

5) The people you meet, know and how they influence you

6) Bosses at work and performance reviews

7) The career positions you obtained and how these positions prepared you for the next targeted position

8) Security and survival needs are most important – not a risk taker

9) Your marital and family situation

10) Your personality (competitive vs. laid back)

11) The need to live in a certain location

12) Your self-image and how others view you

13) Believing in yourself or confidence level

14) Work ethic – willing to work long hours and complete the job

15) Type of lifestyle you want to live

Your Career Aspirations During Specific Times in Your Life

Please review the 15 factors we listed and write out the factors that influenced your career aspirations the most throughout your life. If you can think other factors that are not mentioned, please list them.

High School Years

My *Career Aspiration* was to

become:_____

What factor(s) influenced your decision the most and why?

       a)_____

       b)_____

Post High School Education (trade, technical, undergraduate, graduate, and professional school)

My *Career Aspiration* (is/was) to become _____

What factor(s) influenced your decision the most and why (post secondary education aspirations)?

       a) _____

       b) _____

Your *20's*

My *Career Aspiration* (is/was) to become _____

What factor(s) influenced your decision the most and why?

       a) _____

       b) _____

Your 30's

My *Career Aspiration* (is/was) to become _____

What factor(s) influenced your decision the most and why?

       a) _____

       b) _____

Your 40's

My *Career Aspiration* **(is/was) to become** _____

      What factor(s) influenced your decision the most and why?

          a) _____

          b) _____

Your 50's

My *Career Aspiration* **(is/was) to become** _____

      What factor(s) influenced your decision the most and why?

          a) _____

          b) _____

Your 60's

My *Career Aspiration* **(is/was) to become** _____

What factor(s) influenced your decision the most and why?

          a)_____

          b)_____

Your 70's

My *Career Aspiration* **(is/was) to become** _____

What factor(s) influenced your decision the most and why?

          a)_____

          b)_____

Identify Your Next Targeted Position and Develop the Growth Objectives That Need to be Met to Excel in This Position

Next Targeted Position_____

Your Perceived Responsibilities:

Write several growth objectives after reviewing your *Leadership and Management Competency Survey*. Where do you need to improve?

Write several growth objectives after reviewing your *Group leadership Behavior Assessment*. Where do you need to change?

Write several growth objectives after reviewing your *Team Leadership Assessment*. Where do you need to improve?

Write several growth objectives after reviewing your *Personal Values Assessment*. Where values do you need to reinforce?

Write several growth objectives after reviewing your *Emotional Intelligence Assessment.* Where do you need to improve?

Write several growth objectives after reviewing your *Interpersonal Communication Assessment.* Where do you need to improve?

Write several growth objectives after reviewing your *Performance Management System.* Where do you need to improve?

\

What additional education and training do you need to be effective in your targeted position?

What additional experience do you need to be effective in your next position?

107

Press On.

Nothing in the world can take the place of

persistence.

Ray A. Kroc

Step Five-

Focus on Left Side of the Triangle- The Team Unit Plan

We would like you to complete the following *three tasks* to complete *Step Five.*

"The defining characteristics of a true leader

is that he or she never accepts the world

as it is-but instead always strive to make

the world as it should be"

Condoleeza Rice
Former Secretary of State

***Task One*- Research Your Competition and Have Employees and the other Stakeholders Evaluate Your Organization and Unit/Group**.

(Researching Your Competition)
There are a number of online directories that one can use to find out information on your competition. Three include;

- **Reference U.S.A. -**You can learn the companies size (sales volume and number of employees) location and about their executives).
- **Lexis Nexis-** You can do news searches, legal searches on company searches to gather information..
- **Business Source Premier-**You can do a *SWOT* search on companies. You can learn about their **Strengths, Weaknesses, Opportunities and Threats.**

You can also hire professional groups to provide you with information on your competition so you can develop objectives and action plans.

(Researching Your Customers)
There are many companies that do customer satisfaction surveys periodically to gain feedback on their products and service. You should do it or hire an outside firm to do it for you. The feedback can help you set important objective to grow your business.

(Stakeholder Satisfaction Surveys)
There are many people that are involved with the success of an organization. It is probably a good idea to identify your stakeholders and conduct satisfaction surveys at least once a year so you learn where to make improvements and gain their loyalty and backing. These individuals include;

- Customers
- Employees
- Stockholders/Brokerage Firms/Wall Street
- Suppliers
- Bankers/Investment Firms
- Family Members
- Community Members
- Retirees

111

Employee Evaluation Survey-Below is an evaluation survey that team unit leaders and direct reports can fill out. Team unit leaders and direct reports can discuss the results and set priority objectives for the unit/company and themselves.

40 Major Challenges Facing Your Organization	Please rate the following challenges on how they are managed. Scale 0 – 10 0 – Poorly 10 –Excellent Job
1. Creating change agendas that are needed, communicating the agendas and gaining commitment to implement them.	
2. Developing a Task Empowerment Program to determine where an employee needs coaching or when he/she needs to be empowered.	
3. Attracting, selecting and retaining employees	
4. Establishing a pay for performance incentive plan.	
5. Increasing profit and shareholder value.	
6. Developing a company vision, mission, objectives and a plan and executing the plan so we are successful.	
7. Maintaining excellent relations with present customers while increasing your customer base.	
8. Determining what businesses we want to be in.	
9. Identifying our market niche and increasing market share.	
10. Developing a one-on-one management program to increase individual productivity, performance and leadership so employees and the company become the best in the field.	
11. Pursuing a cause or purpose that will unify, excite and reward everyone in the organization.	
12. Increasing quality of products/service while managing costs.	
13. Training employees how to function as skilled performance facilitators to bring out the best in themselves and others.	
14. Keeping up with the latest technology to remain competitive.	
15. Satisfying and meeting the needs of the workforce so they can better focus on achieving tasks and objectives.	
16. Building a unified workforce	
17. Containing health care costs and decreasing absenteeism at work.	
18. Building a "Competitive Intelligence and Learning Center" to grow individuals and beat the competition.	
19. Deciding whether to manufacture or outsource products.	
20. Establishing a participation management style to include all employees in the business planning process.	
21. Constantly striving to beat local and global competition to be number one in the marketplace.	

22. Defining and living company team values.	
23. Using the expertise of retired employees.	
24. Evaluating how we communicate to each other in the organization and developing a plan to improve communication	
25. Reducing costs by hiring a combination of full time, part time and temporary employees.	
26. Establishing a career development program for all employees.	
27. Identifying performance facilitating behaviors and working with employees to turn them into everyday habits.	
28. Developing a merger and acquisition strategy to grow.	
29. Managing occupational safety and health.	
30. Establishing a program that reduces anger and lawsuits in the workplace.	
31. Developing a competency base program and creating a talent pool to be used through the organization.	
32. Managing downsizing and restructuring without reducing the enthusiasm and commitment of the workforce.	
33. Supplying the resources needed to compete and grow the company while maintaining a meaningful work environment.	
34. Developing a team leadership model so all employees know when and how to step up as leaders.	
35. Defining what is politically and ethically correct in the organization.	
36. Having an effective Board of Directors and senior management team.	
37. Establishing a win-win situation between the union and management.	
38. Identifying future team unit leaders and building a leadership farm system to train them	
39. Helping employees balance work and personal life.	
40. Marketing and selling your company stock analysts & public.	
TOTAL POINTS	=
DIVIDE BY 40 TO OBTAIN SCORE) **AVERAGE SCORE**	=

Unit's Average Score_____

Team Unit leader's Average Score_____

Challenges Facing Our Team Unit and Company

The 5 major challenges facing our unit and company in the next few months are:

Team Unit	Company
1.	1.
2.	2.
3.	3.
4.	4.
5.	5.

Our 5 *projected* major challenges in the next year are:

Team Unit	Company
1.	1.
2.	2.
3.	3.
4.	4.
5.	5.

How are the challenges facing your department different from those of the company?

Sports Teams- A coach would identify the objectives that would need to be met by the team to win a championship. He/she should keep and review important statistics each year to have a starting point for the new objectives.

If you are a sports coach, you would want to break your team up into the appropriate triangles. In football, the first triangle would be the players and coach on offense and they would set objectives. The second triangle would be players and coach on defense and they would set objectives. The third triangle would be the players and coach on the specialty team and they would set objectives. Hopefully, the objectives that are set and achieved, would transform the unit into a championship team and the players into all league or All American status.

In baseball, the first triangle would be the pitchers and catchers and coach who would set objectives. The second triangle would include the infielders and coach that would set objectives and the third triangle would be the outfielders and their coach and they would set objectives.

You always have one triangle with the head coach, assistants and team unit. These individuals always set the overall objectives and pass them down to the team units to gain their endorsement and additional objectives. In basketball, you would have one triangle for the players and head coach and they can set the unit objectives that will win a championship after they hear about the head coach's objectives.

College Campus Group leaders on campus would set champion building or best in our class objectives focusing on grades, graduation timelines, student retention, personal and leadership development, number of internships and job placement. Unit leaders would keep and review important statistics each year to have a starting point for new objectives.

You can take this *Model* to residence halls and fraternities and sororities and have the resident advisors and officers execute it. Each resident advisor and each officer could set a triangle with six or seven individuals in the triangle. College credit could be given to the group leaders for executing the *Triangle Team Leadership Model* with fellow students and achieving important objectives.

**Task Two-** Review the Organization's Vision and Mission Statements and Our Suggested Growth Goals and Objectives for Your Organization and Unit (Division, Department or Group).

We would like you to write out the vision and mission statement of your organization. Then ask yourself do these statements inspire all employees and take into account all other stakeholders?

The CEO and senior management team should establish a vision and mission statement and take into account the legitimate interest of all stakeholders. Your present vision and mission statements are:

Vision Statement:

Mission Statement:

Do these statements inspire all your employees and take in the interest of other stakeholders?

(Samples)

A vision statement for the _Triangle Team Leadership Model_ would be:
"Our company will strive to be an expert leader in the retail industry continually improving our customer base and their satisfaction with our service and products so we are number one in our field. It is by working together as a team and bringing out the best in each other that this vision can be a reality".

A mission statement for the Model would be:
"Everyone associated with the company will work as partners to make our products and services and ourselves the best we can be so our customer base and stock value grows and all stakeholder needs and expectations are met"

Suggested "Best in Our Field" Champion Building/Profitable Objectives

Identify the growth goals you desire and then develop and meet champion building and "best in our field" objectives to move units, the organization and people forward.

Developing the right growth goals along with champion building objectives is considered to be a top priority of the company, unit and a team member. As a start, the *Triangle Team Leadership Model* recommends you review the 13 suggested growth goals below and the champion building objectives illustrated on the next two pages. These growth goals focus on making profit and meeting the needs of stakeholders. They are called the work and life growth goals. Your task is to identify the growth goals you want to concentrate on this coming year to make sure you are the best at what you do.

Goal One -   *Increase Your Income and Cash Flow*
Goal Two-   *Control and Manage Expenses So You Don't Exceed Your Income*
Goal Three-   *Meet the Expectations and Needs of Your Customers and Grow*
                     Your Customer Base
Goal Four-   *Recruit, Develop and Retain Employees Who Will Help You Be*
                   The Best in Your Industry
Goal Five-   *Build a Performance Facilitating Culture, One That Brings Out The*
                   Best in Others so Everyone can be a Champion Performer
Goal Six-   *Meet the Expectations of Your Shareholders*
Goal Seven-   *Meet the Expectations and Needs of Your Suppliers*
Goal Eight-   *Meet the Expectations and Needs of Family Members*
Goal Nine-   *Meet the Expectations and Needs of Retirees*
Goal Ten-   *Help the Local Community in a Positive Way*
Goal Eleven-   *Identify the Strengths of Each Direct Report and Develop a Plan*
                   to Use These Strengths to Achieve the Champion Building Objectives.
Goal Twelve-   *Identify the Anchors (impediments) of Each Direct Report and Create a*
                   Plan to Get Rid of the Anchors Issues.
Goal Thirteen–Meet the Expectations of Colleagues and Other Departments

Before writing objectives, let's discuss the subject of objectives. An objective is specific description of an end result to be achieved. AN EFFECTIVE OBJECTIVE *SHOULD:*
1) be conceivable, believable and achievable
2) be measurable (numbers and times)
3) have a starting and ending time line
4) keep you focused on what and when you must do something
5) contain clear lines of responsibility and authority
6) be flexible so it can be changed at a given moment
7) be clearly understood
8) truly make your organization stand above the competition

The benefits of written objectives are:

*We avoid lapses in memory.
*There are fewer misunderstandings.
*They keep everyone on track: activities should be related to an end result.
*We can be adequately evaluated on results rather than activities.

Examples Objectives
Poor:
Increase sales as much as we can under the circumstances.
Good:
Increase the U.S. sales income in our sports helmet business from $500,000 to $600,000 for a net gain of $100,000 in 201_____.
Poor:
Increase market share to where we can stay in business.
Good:
Increase the U.S. market share in our sports helmet business from 45% to 50% in 201_____.

Implement the *GAP Analysis & Closure Model and Task Empowerment Process* to achieve each unit's objectives: *The GAP Analysis & Closure Model* was developed to help you determine where you are, where you want to go and what tasks or activities you must do to close the gap. *The Task Empowerment Process* will help you identify and execute the tasks necessary to meet objectives to close the *Gap.*

Suggested Company and Unit (Division & Department) Goals and Champion Building Objectives

We will provide champion building objective suggestions for each of the 13 goals previously mentioned. The purpose of this exercise is to provide an opportunity for your company, division and department to identify objectives that might be incorporated in the total champion building objectives package. If the company does not use some of the suggested objectives below and you think they are important, incorporate them into your division or department champion building objectives. Your next challenge would be to define and execute the tasks that will help you and direct reports meet each objective.

Goal One - Increase Your Income and Cash Flow
The corporate objectives could include:
1) Increase total sales income from _____ to _____ for the period beginning January 1 and ending December 31, 20_____.
2) Increase market share in each product/service by ____% for the period beginning January 1 and ending December 31, 20_____.
3) Select products/services with the most profit margin and increase sales in each by _____% in the year 20_____.
4) Increase our total customer base from _____ to _____ for the period beginning January 1 and ending December 31, 20_____.
5) Increase the expert leadership power of every employee and publish a company-wide expert book listing the experts in the organization so you save $_____ in consulting fees and $_____ in loss of employees because they never receive any recognition.
6) Increase net profit by _____% each year.

Goal Two- Control and Manage Expenses So They Don't Exceed Your Income.
1) Develop a budget and aim to reduce it from_____ to _____ in 20_____.
2) Reduce our benefit costs from_____ to _____% in 20_____.
3) Reduce the cost to produce each product by _____% or to deliver a service by _____% in 20____.
4) Reduce absenteeism from _____ to _____ days and cut yearly costs from temporary employment services from _____ to _____ in 20_____.
5) Increase retention of employees by _____% and reduce yearly search fees from_____ to _____ in 20_____.
6) Reduce lawsuits and cut legal expenses from_____ to _____ in 20_____..
7) Increase wellness among employees and reduce medical expenses from_____ to _____ in 20_____..
8) Every employee will cut back on texting, phone and e-mail time to family and friends each day by _____minutes in 20_____.

119

Goal Three- Meet the Expectations and Needs of Your Customers and Grow Your Customer Base

1) Retain existing customers and increase new customers by _____% in 20_____.
2) Identify three services or improvements in products that will retain our customers in 20_____.
3) Identify, develop or buy new products that will expand our customer base.
4) Design a customer satisfaction survey and assess customers twice per year making the appropriate changes to retain customers in 20_____.
5) Create five outrageous new services that will increase the customer base by _____% in 20_____.
6) Establish the Partnership Expectation PAC with customers inside and outside the company and honor each agreement in 20_____.
7) Send out a customer satisfaction survey three days after a service has been rendered and use the information to make the appropriate changes to retain customers in 20____.

Goal Four -*Recruit, Develop and Retain Employees Who Will Help You Be the Best in Your Industry*

1) All employees must meet a minimum of twelve times a year with their team unit leader in One-on-One meetings to set and achieve the champion building objectives.
2) All employees must participate and attend 90% of the team unit meetings and achieve their team unit objectives in 20_____.
3) All employees must develop a career pathing profile and resume so they can be placed in the right position to complete tasks that help the unit meet it's objectives 20_____.
4)The One-on-One champion building plan should meet the three most crucial needs of each employee in 20_____.
5) The One-on-One champion building plan should address three areas where individuals are most dissatisfied and eliminate them in 20_____.
6) The One-on-One partnership meetings will discuss the topics of change, stress and anxiety, weight, health and how individuals can better manage these issues in 20_____.
7) Each employee must be competent in:
- Setting objectives and identifying the tasks needed to be complete to meet the objectives.
- Technical knowledge and skills
- Career planning, development and placement
- Operating as a performance facilitator
- Understanding group dynamics and how teams succeed and fail

Each employee will be expected to participate in the *Performance Triangle Leadership Model* and help their team members, department, division and company achieve their champion building objectives.

120

Goal Five- Build a Performance Facilitating Culture, One That Brings Out The Best In Others To Be Champion Performers

1) 100% of employees should review the company vision and mission statements, discuss them, and commit to them in 20_____.

2) At least 90% of the employees should approve the corporate growth goals and champion building objectives and commit to them in 20_____.

3) The individual and team champion building objectives should be established and met by everyone on the team in 20_____.

4) All executives, managers and supervisors must learn the Performance Triangle Leadership model and how to be effective in the one-on-one and team unit meetings to build a championship team.

5) Each team unit will adopt a number of guiding themes that will take the unit as far and high as they want to go.

6) The company will develop a number of performance facilitating behaviors and have each person on the team turn them in to every day habits. Each person will be evaluated on these behaviors in one-on-one meetings with their team unit leader twice a year and during their team unit meetings.

7) Performance facilitating work rules (bringing out the best in each other) should be written and carried out to facilitate performance, build a positive work environment and retain employees.

8) Everyone in the organization will be assessed as a skilled helper and performance facilitator and trained as one in the year 20_____.

Goal Six-   Meet the Expectations of Your Shareholders

1) Increase dividends to stock holders from_____ to _____ in 20_____.

2) Meet the earnings projections, and develop a strategy to sell the stock analysts and public on buying our company stock so it goes from _____ to _____ in 20_____.

Goal Seven- Meet the Expectations of Your Suppliers

Identify the three expectations of suppliers, develop a plan and meet them in 20_____.

Meet with your suppliers _____ times per year to establish rapport and give them an evaluation report on their products and services.

3) Pay your suppliers within _____days so they don't go out of business.

Goal Eight- Meet the Needs and Expectations of Family Members

1) Identify the two most crucial needs of you family members, develop a plan and meet their needs in 20_____.

2) Identify what your spouse, and children expect from you and meet these expectations in 20_____.

3) Develop a "Parent's Mentoring" Program at work to help parents be more effective in helping their children succeed in school, life and work and be out the house by age 30.

Goal Nine- *Meet the Expectations and Needs of Retired Employees*

1) Identify the two most crucial needs of retired employees, develop a plan and meet the need in 20_____.
2) Identify where you need help in your company and hire some retired employees back part time.
3) Identify what your retired employees expect from you and try to meet these expectations in 20____.
4) If you establish a mentoring program, hire ___ retirees to serve as mentors in 20___.

Goal Ten- **Help the Local Community in a Positive Way**

1) Each employee will participate in one community project in 20_____.
2) Make a list of actions that your company could do to help your local community in 20____.

Goal Eleven- **Identify the Strengths of Each Direct Report and Develop a Plan For Them to Use Their Strengths to Achieve the Champion Building Objectives**

1) Team members should participate in the *Team Engagement Achievement Motivation* Program and identify each person's strengths on the team based on their past successes.
2).The team members should fill out a number of relevant assessments surveys and identify their strengths so they know their potential.

Goal Twelve- **Identify the Weaknesses or Anchor Issues of Each Direct Report and Create a Plan to Transform the Identified Weaknesses into Strengths.**

1) The team members will go through the *Team Engagement Achievement Motivation Program* and identify the weaknesses that need to be changed into strengths..
2).The team members will take a number of relevant assessments and identify their weaknesses and develop a plan to turn the weaknesses into strengths.

Goal Thirteen--**Meet Expectations of Work Colleagues and Fellow Department Heads**

) You will identify and meet with important work colleagues outside your department and with fellow department heads and draw up a *Partner Expectation Pac* with a list of what you can expect from each other .
2) You will meet quarterly with these important work colleagues and department heads and grade yourselves on how you are meeting each others expectations.

Corporate Champion Building Objectives
Group Dialogue and Action
Which of the champion building objectives would you delete from each goal?

Which champion building objectives would you add to each goal?

Write out your final champion building objectives in *Step Seven* and turn them into the organization's Performance Evaluation Committee.

Task Three- Write a Vision and Mission Statement and "Best in Our
 Field "Objectives for Your Organization or Unit Based On Your Leadership
Position in the Organization.

**Before you write the vision and mission statements, growth goals and championship
building objectives for your division and department, make sure you know the final
list of the champion building objectives for the corporation. This will help you stay
on target when you write your division and department objectives.**

Your Unit Vision

Your Unit Mission Statement

<u>**Write Champion Building Objectives for Each Goal**</u>

<u>Goal One</u> - _Increase Your Income and Cash Flow_

1)

2)

3)

Write Champion Building Objectives Below for Each Goal

Goal Two- _Control and Manage Expenses So You Don't Exceed Your Income_

1)

2)

3)

Goal Three- _Meet the Expectations and Needs of Your Customers and Grow Your Customer Base_

1)

2)

3)

Goal Four- _Recruit, Develop and Retain Employees Who Will Help You Be The Best in Your Industry_

1)

2)

3)

Write Champion Building Objectives Below for Each Goal

Goal Five- ***Build a Performance Facilitating Culture, One That Brings Out The Best In Others To Be Champion Performers***

1)

2)

3)

Goal Six- ***Meet the Expectations of Your Shareholders***
List Champion Building Objectives Below

1)

2)

3)

Goal Seven- ***Meet the Expectations and Needs of Your Suppliers***
List Champion Building Objectives Below

1)

2)

3)

Write Champion Building Objectives Below for Each Goal

**Goal Eight**- Meet the Needs and Expectations of Family Members

1)

2)

3)

**Goal Nine**- Meet the Expectations and Needs of Retired Employees

1)

2)

3)

Goal Ten- Help the Local Community in a Positive Way
List Champion Building Objectives Below

1)

2)

3)

Write Champion Building Objectives Below for Each Goal

Goal Eleven- Identify the Strengths of Each Direct Report and Develop a Plan for Them to Use Their Strengths to Achieve the Champion Building Objectives

1.)

2)

3)

4)

Goal Twelve- Identify the Weaknesses and Anchor Issues of Each Direct Report and Create a Plan to Transform Them into Strengths

1.)

2.)

3.)

4)

Goal Thirteen--Meet Expectations of Colleagues and Fellow Department Heads

1)

2)

3)

127

List additional growth goals and champion building objectives below that would be important for your division or department to execute.

SUGGESTED GROWTH GOALS FOR SPORTS TEAMS-YOU CAN ADD OTHER GOALS

*OUR TEAM WILL WIN MORE GAMES THAN OUR COMPETITION.
* WE WILL HAVE MORE CHAMPION PERFORMERS THAN PLAYERS ON THE OTHER TEAMS
* WE WILL SCORE MORE THAN THE OPPOSITION.
* WE WILL ALLOW FEWER POINTS PER GAME AND FOR YEAR THAN ANY TEAM IN LEAGUE

SUGGESTED GROWTH GOALS FOR COLLEGE STUDENTS-YOU CAN ADD OTHER GOALS

*WE WILL GRADUATE FROM COLLEGE ON OUR TIME LINE WITH _____DEBT
*WE WILL ASSESS OURSELVES AS A SELF MANAGER AND BECOME ONE
*WE WILL ASSESS OURSELVES AS CAREER MANAGERS AND BECOME ONE
*WE WILL BECOME AWARE OF OURSELVES AND THE WORLD OF WORK AND SELECT A
   CAREER FIELD AND COLLEGE MAJOR THAT IS A GOOD FIT.
*WE WILL EXECUTE A JOB SEARCH PROCESS THAT WILL LAND US A GOOD JOB AT
   COLLEGE GRADUATION

ORDER *THE FIVE GOAL COLLEGE PLAN* WHICH COVERS THESE FIVE GOALS AT
WWW.MULLIGANASSOC.COM

Step Six-

Focus on the Right Side of the Triangle-The Team Members' Plans

We would like you to complete the following *two tasks* to complete *Step Six*.

Page

Task One- Review Unit Objectives with Each Direct Report to Gain Their Endorsement and Ideas for Other Growth Objectives.

Goal One - *Increase Your Income and Cash Flow*

1)

2)

3)

Goal Two- *Control and Manage Expenses So You Don't Exceed Your Income*

1)

2)

3)

Goal Three- *Meet the Expectations and Needs of Your Customers and Grow Your Customer Base*

1)

2)

3)

Goal Four- Recruit, Develop and Retain Employees Who Will Help You Be The Best in Your Industry

1)

2)

3)

Goal Five- Build a Performance Facilitating Culture, One That Brings Out The Best In Others To Be Champion Performers

1)

2)

3)

Goal Six- Meet the Expectations of Your Shareholders
List Champion Building Objectives Below

1)

2)

3)

Goal Seven *- Meet the Expectations and Needs of Your Suppliers*
List Champion Building Objectives Below

1)

2)

3)

 Goal Eight *- Meet the Needs and Expectations of Family Members*

1)

2)

Goal Nine *- Meet the Expectations and Needs of Retired Employees*

1)

2)

Goal Ten **- Help the Local Community in a Positive**

1)

2)

<u>Goal Eleven</u>- Identify the Strengths of Each Direct Report and Develop a Plan for Them to Use Their Strengths to Achieve the Champion Building Objectives

1.)

2)

3)

4)

<u>Goal Twelve</u>- Identify the Anchors Holding Back the Performance of Each Direct Report and Create a Plan to Eliminate Them

1.)

2.)

3.)

4)

<u>Goal Thirteen</u>--Meet Expectations of Colleagues and Fellow Department Heads

1)

2)

3)

Ask direct reports to list additional growth goals and champion building objectives below that would be important for your division or department to execute.

Task Two -Assess Direct Reports and Meet One-On-One to Review Their Results and Write Personal "Best in Our Field" Objectives

The following *20 assessments* can provide information that can help unit leaders transform direct reports into champion performers or best in their field. If unit leaders have direct reports that are in management, they can use the assessments in Step Four of this book. If direct reports are not in management, unit leaders can order the book *The Team Members' Plans* which has additional assessments. Call Mulligan & Associates at 847 981-5725.

1. The Strategic Leadership Program-Using the Leadership Effectiveness Analysis Survey – A 360 degree program developed by *The Management Research Group*. Helps team leaders identify and understand their weaknesses and strengths on 22 leadership traits. This is a good tool for a high level unit leader use with direct reports that are unit leaders. This program help all team unit leaders put into practice the leadership behaviors most important in helping the unit or organization move forward.

2. The Mulligan Leadership Personality Profile-Measures eight personality leadership traits (competitiveness, determination, self directed, organized, patient, helper, innovative and team builder) that are important in being a team unit leader, team member leader and manager. Designed to place people in the right leadership positions and help them develop a growth plan so they can carry out both leadership roles when placed in the situation. It can be completed by both the individual and boss if one desires a contrast.

3. The Leadership and Manager Competency Survey-Measures a person's competency level to carry out 20 leadership and 40 management tasks. The results can be used in a leadership and management development program.

4. The Career Management Competency Survey – A 100 item career management survey that tells an individual where they need the most help in managing their career. This survey also tells a manager the areas where his direct reports need the most help in managing their career.

5. The Work Tasks & Leadership Skills Assessment Survey- One hears all the time that he/she does not have the skill set for the job. This survey helps people identify their top skills so they can place themselves in the right positions.

6. The Group Dynamics Assessment Survey- Reveals one's behavior in leading and being a member of a group. You can study the dynamics of the group.

7. The Performance Facilitator Assessment Survey- Measures the functioning level of a person in five performance facilitation areas. A growth plan can be developed to help an individual operate as a performance facilitator in his/her culture. This survey can be completed by an individual and boss if a contrast is desired.

Assessment Surveys Continued

8. The Interpersonal Communication Assessment Survey - a survey that measures where a person is functioning when it comes to interacting and helping people understand problems and issues and making appropriate plans to solve their issues and problems. Effective communication in an organization is key to having engaged employees and helping each other succeed. Seven out of 10 people are operating at a harmful level when helping others make decisions, solve issues and be successful. Completed by individual and boss if you desire a contrast.

9. E.Q. Assessment Survey a survey that measures one's emotional intelligence – a key ingredient to being a successful leader and human being. Completed by individual and boss if you desire a contrast.

10. The Route 66 Job Satisfaction Survey - a survey that measures an employee's satisfaction with the career route they are own at this time.. This information is necessary to increase performance, work satisfaction and retention.

11. The Self Actualization Assessment Survey- a survey that measures five basic needs of employees. The thinking is if the security, survival and belonging needs of a person are being met, they can then focus on the challenges at hand using their full potential to become and be the best at what they do. They become self actualized and operate at a peak performance. This information is Important to increasing performance, bringing out the talent in people and retaining top talent.

12. The 21 Personal Values Assessment Survey- a survey that ranks 21 values of an individual and provides both an individual and team report. If the values of people on a team are too far apart, there could be dissonance on the team with out knowing why.

13. The Work Values Preference Survey- A survey that ranks five work values and tells one what an individual values most about work.

14. The Group Leadership Assessment Survey- a survey that helps those leading groups understand where they are functioning when it comes to using relationship and task behavior in building high performance teams.

15. The Coping Skills Assessment Survey – a survey that measure one's capability to cope with different situations and issues at work.

16. The Consultant Assessment Survey*- helps an individual understand whether or not he or she will enjoy doing consulting work

Assessment Surveys Continued

17. The Entrepreneur Assessment Survey- a survey on being an entrepreneur. Helps people understand what an entrepreneur looks like and if they look like one.

18. DiSC- measures four primary behaviors of a person- Dominance, Influencing, Steady or Compliant- generates a 30 page report- a great tool to help you place people in the right positions and understand direct reports and help them grow. Helps individuals understand themselves-overall personality profile, what motivates them, their preferred work environment, how they interact with people and how they like to be managed.

19.. Myers Briggs Type Indicator- (MBTI) a personality assessment that places a person in one of 16 personality categories.. Helps people understand their personality traits- a good tool to use to understand yourself, other individuals and the group dynamics of your group or team unit.

20. Jackson Vocational Interest Survey- an interest inventory that can help individuals learn what they might like to study in college or career fields that they might like to enter

After reviewing these 20 assessment surveys, list below the ones you would like to have your direct reports fill out.

Evaluate the performance of your team unit and direct reports

We would like you to rate your team units' overall performance and if your direct reports are meeting your expectations.

Please use the following rating scale to evaluate your team unit and the members:

5	Exceeded my expectations
4	Better than I expected
3	Met my expectations
2	Slightly missed my expectations
1	Failed my expectations

List the priority objectives of your team unit. Rate how your team unit perfromed last year and is doing this year.

Last year/ This year

1. _____ Rating _____ _____

_____

2. _____ Rating _____ _____

_____

3. _____ Rating _____ _____

_____

4. _____ Rating _____ _____

_____

5. _____ Rating _____ _____

_____

6. _____ Rating _____ _____

_____

Which objectives did your team fail to meet last year? Why did the team unit fail to achieve the objectives?

1. _____

2. _____

3. _____

List your boss and the members of your team unit below and rate them overall on how they met your expectations last year and how they are doing this year.

5   Exceeded my expectations
4   Better than I expected
3   Met my expectation
2   Slightly missed my expectations
1   Failed my expectations

                                                          Last year/This year

Boss   _____   Rating _____ _____

1) Direct Report _____   Rating _____ _____

2) Direct Report _____   Rating _____ _____

3) Direct Report _____   Rating _____ _____

4) Direct Report _____   Rating _____ _____

5) Direct Report _____   Rating _____ _____

6) Direct Report _____   Rating _____ _____

7) Direct Report _____   Rating _____ _____

8) Direct Report _____   Rating _____ _____

                                          Total Score   _____ _____
                                          Mean Score   _____ _____

Who are your two top performers?

1)_____ 2)_____

Who are your two bottom performers?

1)_____ 2)_____

139

Use The Task Empowerment Process with Direct Reports

Preparing Your Direct Reports to Carry Out Specific Tasks to Meet
Champion Building Objectives and Become an Expert Task Leader

In chapter two of this workbook, Dr. Mulligan defined two types of leadership. The first is the *team unit leader*. This is where one has to bring all direct reports together to work as a team. All assigned to the team unit will be asked to establish growth goals and champion building objectives for the team as well as themselves. The main challenge for the team unit leader is that he/she has to work with and through all direct reports to meet the established objectives. The team unit leader must be able and willing to implement specific tasks to help individuals meet their objectives as well as the objectives of the unit.

The second type of leader is the *team member leader*. The team unit leader will sit down with each team member and review the team unit's objectives first. Then the team unit leader and team member will establish individual objectives ,that if achieved, will help the team unit and team member become the best in their field. Team members will be asked to develop an action plan that show the tasks they must implement to achieve their individual objectives. The team member must be able and willing to implement these specific tasks if they and the unit are going to be successful.

The goal is to help the team unit leader and team member leader become an expert in implementing the tasks that are necessary for them to be successful. To become an expert at implementing certain tasks, one has to gain knowledge, skills and experience. The more a person demonstrates expertise in implementing the tasks, the more they will be empowered and given position power or authority to do the tasks alone or teach others.

In Step Six, we would like to demonstrate the *Task Empowerment Process,* a model a team unit leader can use with direct reports when meeting one on one. We will explain the *Task Empowerment Process* on the following pages. During this process, the team unit leader working with the team member will play the role of a mentor/helper (adviser, counselor and coach).

As team unit leaders meet with their direct reports to determine their preparation and commitment to perform tasks to meet specific objectives, the communication style will vary based on the readiness level of the individual to perform certain tasks. There are five levels of task leadership readiness and you should know the readiness level of your direct reports to perform each task. This knowledge is gained through one-on-one discussions and observations of the direct report. Identifying the readiness level of your direct reports to perform certain task calls for various communication styles which facilitates higher levels of performance.

The five task leadership readiness levels are:

Level	Task Readiness	Communication Style
Five	*An (Expert) at Completing Task* (can train others)	*Positive Reinforcement* (The Best of the Best)
Four	Able and Willing to Complete Task (prepared and committed to task) -unconsciously competent-(Task Master)	*Empowered* (you can do it)
Three	Able but Not Willing to Complete Task (prepared but not committed to task) -consciously competent-	*Counseling* (need more discussion)
Two	Willing but Not Able to Complete Task (not prepared but committed to training) -consciously incompetent-	*Coaching* (teaching the tasks)
One	Identifying Tasks to Complete (not prepared and not committed) -unconsciously incompetent-	*Coaching/advising* (Identifying what needs to be done to be successful)

In **Level One**, the mentor/manager and direct report identify the tasks that are necessary to complete in order to achieve the predetermined objectives. The mentor/manager and direct report must discuss the tasks and then the direct report must identify the level where he/she is functioning in regard to task leadership readiness. The team mentor/manager uses an appropriate communication style based on the direct report's readiness level. At level one, the direct report learns about the task and is not ready to perform the task. Thus, the team unit leader can be more direct serving as an adviser/coach

In **Level Two**, the preparation stage, the mentor/manager uses a coaching/teaching approach. The direct report knows he or she is not competent to achieve specific tasks and is willing to be taught or trained in these areas to reach a level 4 or 5. At level 4, you become empowered and at Level 5, you are classified as an expert. The identification of good tutors and coaches is important and training must be completed.

In **Level Three**, the commitment stage, the mentor/manager uses a counseling approach. The direct report is prepared but needs to discuss the situation more thoroughly before moving forward. He or she might need to review where they are and need a little more encouragement and understanding before they are ready to implement the task alone.

In **Level Four**, the empowerment stage, the team unit leader gives full authority to the direct report to perform the task alone. The direct report is both prepared and committed and can do the task by himself/herself. As direct reports continue to complete the task by themselves, they become unconsciously competent. They can do it without thinking about how to do it. The team unit leader moves from being a micromanager to a micromanager. The direct report can do the task alone.

In **Level Five**, the expert stage, the mentor/manager uses the positive reinforcement approach so the individual feels good about his accomplishment and will repeat the same behavior over and over. We want to encourage the direct report to use what he/she has learned to help someone else. The direct report moves from being a person who needs help to an expert task helper. In essence, the person is perceived as a leader in performing specific tasks.

Establishing The Core Conditions to Reach Level 5 "Unconsciously Competent"

We want all direct reports to move forward to become an expert leader at performing the specific tasks that are needed to meet predetermined objectives. Tasks need to be established and four conditions need to exist for your direct reports to be successful. The four core conditions are:

- **The Four M's Management System**
- **One on One Sessions**
- **Coaching Confrontation**
- **Positive Reinforcement Communication**

The Four M' Management System

As the direct report begins to implement tasks and moves toward meeting the objectives, the mentor/manager will be:

- Monitoring the direct reports readiness to perform all tasks
- Measuring the direct reports efforts and progress
- Modifying or changing the direct reports tasks based on new information
- Meeting the predetermined objectives by helping the direct report implement and achieve the identified tasks.

One-on-One sessions

Team unit leaders should meet or talk with their direct report once a month to discuss the Four M's, confront them , and provide positive reinforcement . The one-on-one sessions will keep everyone focused on the objectives and the tasks that need to be implemented to meet the predetermined objectives.

Constructive Confrontation Coaching

The word "confrontation" is often associated with the stripping away of a person's defenses and brutally exposing his or her weaknesses. The *Leadership Empowerment and Expert Program* advocates constructive coaching confrontation. It is not punitive and cruel. Constructive coaching confrontation helps the individual examine the inconsistencies in his or her work/life. Individuals aren't walking the talk. He/she can start to focus again to make better use of his or her personal strengths and resources. The coach disciplines the person for his present behavior and attitude and wants the person to know they are still loved and appreciated. The team unit leader shows respect to his/her direct reports by believing they will do what they say they are going to do.

Confrontation without an established working relationship is rarely helpful. The model emphasizes that you must earn the right to confront and this is done through building relationships. Confrontation can be damaging and threatening, and create high levels of anxiety. However, anyone who has played sports knows a coach wants to make you better and this requires focusing on both strengths and weaknesses.

Positive Reinforcement Communication

Just as it is important to point out discrepancies in performance, it is important to recognize excellent work and provide positive feedback on a timely basis. When an individual completes a task or project, meets predetermined objectives or behaves in a certain way to facilitate performance in others, the person should be complimented or recognized. Positive reinforcement should be done on an intermittent basis. This means people should be rewarded or praised at different times without expecting it. If we reward or praise someone all the time, it doesn't mean as much. The problem is that people aren't praised or recognized enough.

On the following pages, we will set up a page to illustrate how to use the Leadership Empowerment and Expert Program with direct reports.

Some sample champion building objectives are written out below.

1. I will master and perform four special tasks to help the company increase it's income   from $_____ to $_____ in 20 ____ . .

2. I will master and perform three special tasks to help my department decrease it's expenses from $_____ to $_____ in 20 ____ . .

3. I will master and perform three special tasks to increase our customer satisfaction rating from _____ to _____ in 20_____ . .

The Task Empowerment Process

You will work with your direct reports to help them identify the objectives they need to meet in 20____ to help themselves become a champion performer and the team unit a championship organization. You will list the tasks your direct reports need to complete to achieve specified objectives. You as the team unit leader needs to know the readiness level of each direct report to perform each task. You and your direct report need to rank his/her readiness level for each task using the following scale.

5)-Expert 4)-Need to be Empowered 3)- Not willing 2)- Not Able 1)-Task Identification

Objective One- I will perform the following four tasks to help the company increase it's income from_____ to _____ in 20_____.

Task One-
Task Two-
Task Three-
Task Four-

Objective Two- I will perform the following three tasks to help my department decrease it's expenses from_____ to_____ in 20_____..

Task One-
Task Two-
Task Three-

Objective Three- I will perform the following three tasks to help increase the customer satisfaction score from _____ to _____ in 20____.

Task One-
Task Two-
Task Three-

Team unit leaders should use the *Gap Analysis & Closure Model* to close the starting points and ending points of each objective. The tasks are the activities which help close the gaps. We will review the *Gap Analysis & Closure Model* again.

The Gap Analysis & Closure Model:
(Seven Steps)

Step 1:   Understanding the 20_____ baseline results before establishing the 20_____ objectives- where are we today or at the end of 20____

Step 2:   Determining the 20____ objectives - where we want to be at the end of 20.

Step 3:   Understanding the gap between - where we were in December 20 ___ and where we want to be in December 20 ___.

Step 4:   Visualizing the tasks that need to be completed to close the gap. Can we do it with our existing processes, products, services, and resources?

Step 5:   If we cannot close the gap with our existing processes, products, services, and resources and sales force, what additional products, services, and resources and manpower will we need?

Step 6:   Are we progressing toward meeting our 20____ objectives? What check points, controls or scorecards do we have in place to ensure success?

Step 7:   Identify who is in charge of specific tasks making sure certain individuals know they are accountable for specific results.

PERSONAL GROWTH OBJECTIVES FOR DIRECT REPORTS

DIRECT REPORT # ONE

1.

2.

3.

4.

5.

DIRECT REPORT # TWO

1.

2.

3.

4.

5.

PERSONAL GROWTH OBJECTIVES FOR DIRECT REPORTS

DIRECT REPORT # THREE

1.

2.

3.

4.

5.

DIRECT REPORT # FOUR

1.

2.

3.

4.

5.

PERSONAL GROWTH OBJECTIVES FOR DIRECT REPORTS

DIRECT REPORT # FIVE

1.

2.

3.

4.

5.

DIRECT REPORT # SIX

1.

2.

3.

4.

5.

PERSONAL GROWTH OBJECTIVES FOR DIRECT REPORTS

DIRECT REPORT # SEVEN

1.

2.

3.

4.

5.

DIRECT REPORT # EIGHT

1.

2.

3.

4.

5.

Step Seven

Establish a Performance Evaluation Team and Finalize the Objectives that Need to be Achieved to be Branded the Best

We would like you to complete the following *four tasks* in *Step Seven.*

150

Task One- Establish a Performance Evaluation Team to Observe Your Team Unit in Action

ONE OF THE MAJOR MOTIVATORS OF PEOPLE IS "SHOWING THEM ATTENTION". WHEN THEY TALK AND YOU LISTEN, THEY WANT TO TALK MORE. WHEN THEY TALK AND YOU DON'T LISTEN, THEY WANT TO TALK LESS. WHEN YOU WATCH, LISTEN AND PAY ATTENTION TO SOMEONE, IT MOTIVATES THEM TO EXCEL AT WHAT THEY DO. PEOPLE IN SPORTS PLAY BETTER WHEN THEY ARE WATCHED BY A LARGE CROWD.

THE EARLY HAWTHORNE STUDIES REINFORCED THE "NEED FOR ATTENTION" CONCEPT. THE STUDY INVOLVED THREE SHIFTS AT A PLANT. A CONTEST WAS SET UP TO SEE HOW MUCH EACH SHIFT COULD PRODUCE. EACH SHIFT TRIED TO OUTPERFORM THE NEXT AND THEY DID. WHEN THEY EVALUATED WHY THE EMPLOYEES PERFORMED SO WELL, IT WAS BECAUSE OF THE ATTENTION THEY RECEIVED FROM THE SENIOR MANAGEMENT TEAM. SOMEONE WHO WAS HELD IN HIGH ESTEEM PAID ATTENTION TO THEM.

WHEN YOU AS THE UNIT LEADER CHOOSE A PERFORMANCE EVALUATION TEAM, YOU MIGHT WANT TO SELECT FIVE OR SIX PEOPLE WHO ARE HELD IN HIGH ESTEEM BY YOUR DIRECT REPORTS. YOU CAN EVEN ASK THEM WHO THEY WANT ON THE PERFORMANCE EVALUATION TEAM.

SOME OF THE PEOPLE COULD BE:

> ➤ YOUR BOSS
> ➤ DEPARTMENT HEADS THAT WORK CLOSELY WITH YOUR UNIT
> ➤ SEVERAL CUSTOMERS
> ➤ SOMEONE FROM HUMAN RESOURCES
> ➤ A FAMILY SPOUSE
> ➤ RETIRED EMPLOYEES WHO WORKED IN THE UNIT AT ONE TIME
> ➤ A CONSULTANT
> ➤ AN I.T. PERSON WHO COULD SET UP A SYSTEM TO TRACK THE PERFORMANCE OF INDIVIDUALS AND THE UNIT.

You want people on the Performance Evaluation Team that can make the process fun as well as competitive.

Task Two- **Review Step Two and Finalize Your Personal Champion Building Objectives and Meet Them**

Write out your final objectives below and type them in your computer making sure you have a starting and ending date for each. Please make sure they are measurable and use the *Gap Analysis and Closure* Concept if possible. Put a check mark by the objective when you meet it.

Your goal to be branded "Best in Your Field" is to meet objectives that are listed under three areas; personable, unit and direct reports. Your task here is to set personable growth objectives and meet them.

Review **Step Four**, analyze your assessment results in the areas below and finalize your personal champion building objectives.

> ➤ 21 Leadership Behaviors
> ➤ 60 Leadership and Management Competency Areas
> ➤ Eight Leadership Personality Traits
> ➤ Group Behavior
> ➤ Team Leadership
> ➤ E.Q.
> ➤ One-On-One Interpersonal Communication
> ➤ Performance Management System
> ➤ Education, Credentials and Experience Needed for Present or Next Position
> ➤ Planning Skills
> ➤ Anchor Issues or Problems Holding You Back.

Create 12 Champion Building Objectives for Yourself and List the Tasks You Need to Complete to Meet Objectives. Check Off When Completed.

_____**Objective # 1.**

Task #1-

Task #2-

Task #3-

_____Objective # 2.

Task #1-

Task #2-

Task #3-

_____Objective # 3.

Task #1-

Task #2-

Task #3-

_____Objective # 4.

Task #1-

Task #2-

Task #3-

_____Objective # 5.

Task #1-

Task #2-

Task #3-

____Objective # 6.

Task #1-

Task #2-

Task #3-

____Objective # 7.

Task #1-

Task #2-

Task #3-

____Objective # 8.

Task #1-

Task #2-

Task #3-

____Objective # 9.

Task #1-

Task #2-

Task #3-

____Objective # 10.

Task #1-

Task #2-

Task #3-

____Objective # 11.

Task #1-

Task #2-

Task #3-

____Objective # 12.

Task #1-

Task #2-

Task #3-

Task Three- Review *Step Five*, Finalize the Units' Championship Building Objectives and Work with Direct Reports to Meet Them.

Write out your final unit objectives below under the Goal and type the objectives in your computer making sure you have a starting and ending date for each. Please make sure they are measurable and use the *Gap Analysis and Closure Concept* if possible. **Put a check mark by the objective when you meet it.**

Your goal to be branded "Best in Your Field" is to meet objectives that are listed under three areas; personable, **unit** and direct reports. Your task here is to set growth objectives for the unit and meet them.

Review **Step Five**, analyze the objectives you wrote and finalize them below. Identify which direct reports you want to be accountable for each objective being achieved.

We will list the 14 growth goals again plus room for others. You can write in the final objectives under each growth goal or others.

Goal One - *Increase Your Income and Cash Flow*

Goal Two- *Control and Manage Expenses So You Don't Exceed Your Income*

Goal Three- *Meet the Expectations and Needs of Your Customers and Grow Your Customer Base*

Goal Four- *Recruit, Develop and Retain Employees Who Will Help You Be The Best in Your Industry*

Goal Five- *Build a Performance Facilitating Culture, One That Brings Out The Best In Others To Be Champion Performers*

Goal Six- *Meet the Expectations of Your Shareholders*

Goal Seven- *Meet the Expectations and Needs of Your Suppliers*

Goal Eight- *Meet the Needs and Expectations of Family Members*

Goal Nine- *Meet the Expectations and Needs of Retired Employees*

Goal Ten- Help the Local Community in a Positive Way

Goal Eleven-   Identify the Strengths of Each Direct Report and Develop a Plan for Them to Use Their Strengths to Achieve the Champion Building Objectives

Goal Twelve-   Identify the Anchor Issues Holding Back Each Direct Report and Create a Plan to Help Them Lose the Anchor Issues or Problems.

Goal Thirteen--Meet Expectations of Colleagues and Fellow Department Heads

Goal Fourteen- Identify educational programs that can help direct reports grow.

Goal Fifteen-

WRITE OUT A GOAL AND TWO OBJECTIVES BELOW THAT RELATE TO THE GOAL. DESIGNATE A DIRECT REPORT TO BE ACCOUNTABLE FOR THE UNIT ACHIEVING EACH OBJECTIVE. THE DIRECT REPORT IN CHARGE CAN WRITE OUT TASKS THAT NEED TO BE MET TO ACHIEVE OBJECTIVE WITH YOU, THE UNIT LEADER.

GOAL #ONE-

OBJECTIVE# ONE-

*DIRECT REPORT IN CHARGE*_____

OBJECTIVE # TWO

*DIRECT REPORT IN CHARGE*_____

GOAL #TWO

OBJECTIVE# ONE-

DIRECT REPORT IN CHARGE_____

OBJECTIVE # TWO

DIRECT REPORT IN CHARGE_____

GOAL #THREE

OBJECTIVE# ONE-

DIRECT REPORT IN CHARGE_____

OBJECTIVE # TWO

DIRECT REPORT IN CHARGE_____

GOAL #FOUR

OBJECTIVE# ONE-

DIRECT REPORT IN CHARGE_____

OBJECTIVE # TWO

DIRECT REPORT IN CHARGE_____

GOAL # FIVE

OBJECTIVE# ONE-

DIRECT REPORT IN CHARGE_____

OBJECTIVE # TWO

DIRECT REPORT IN CHARGE_____

GOAL # SIX

OBJECTIVE# ONE-

DIRECT REPORT IN CHARGE_____

OBJECTIVE # TWO

DIRECT REPORT IN CHARGE_____

GOAL # SEVEN

OBJECTIVE# ONE-

DIRECT REPORT IN CHARGE_____

OBJECTIVE # TWO

DIRECT REPORT IN CHARGE_____

GOAL # EIGHT

OBJECTIVE# ONE-

*DIRECT REPORT IN CHARGE*_____

OBJECTIVE # TWO

*DIRECT REPORT IN CHARGE*_____

GOAL # NINE

OBJECTIVE# ONE-

*DIRECT REPORT IN CHARGE*_____

OBJECTIVE # TWO

*DIRECT REPORT IN CHARGE*_____

GOAL # 10

OBJECTIVE# ONE-

DIRECT REPORT IN CHARGE_____

OBJECTIVE # TWO

DIRECT REPORT IN CHARGE_____

GOAL # 11

OBJECTIVE# ONE-

DIRECT REPORT IN CHARGE_____

OBJECTIVE # TWO

DIRECT REPORT IN CHARGE_____

GOAL # 12

OBJECTIVE# ONE-

DIRECT REPORT IN CHARGE_____

OBJECTIVE # TWO

DIRECT REPORT IN CHARGE_____

GOAL # 13

OBJECTIVE# ONE-

DIRECT REPORT IN CHARGE_____

OBJECTIVE # TWO

DIRECT REPORT IN CHARGE_____

Task Four- **Review Step Six and Finalize Direct Reports' Champion Building Objectives and Work with Each Direct Report to Help Them Meet Them.**

We recommend you write the names of each direct report, their personal growth objectives and the unit objectives they are accountable for achieving. You can then meet with each direct report and identify the tasks they need to complete to meet their assigned personal and unit objectives. You need to put all this information in your computer and track the success of each report.

Name of Direct Report #1
Personal Objectives:

(Direct Report #1 Continued)
Unit Objectives:

Name of Direct Report #2
Personal Objectives:

(Direct Report #2 Continued)
Unit Objectives:

Name of Direct Report #3
Personal Objectives:

(Direct Report #3 Continued)
Unit Objectives:

Name of Direct Report #4
Personal Objectives:

(Direct Report #4 Continued)
Unit Objectives:

Name of Direct Report #5
Personal Objectives:

(Direct Report # 5 Continued)
Unit Objectives:

Name of Direct Report #6
Personal Objectives:

(Direct Report # 6 Continued)
Unit Objectives:

Name of Direct Report #7
Personal Objectives:

(Direct Report # 7 Continued)
Unit Objectives:

Special Notes

Bibliography

i   Human Resources Institute of Eckland College, St. Petersburg, Florida, 2006 Study

ii "The Leadership Industry' *Fortune Magazine, February 21, 2006 Issue*

iii Kotter, John. *The Leadership Factor, The Free Press, 1988.*

iv Kotter, John. A Force of Change: How Leadership Differs from Management, Harvard Business Press, 1990.

v "Leadership Styles That Make CEOs" Korn Ferry Study in August 10, 2006. *USA Today*

vi "Superior CEOs" Fortune Magazine, June 21, 2005.

vii McCall, John and Lombardo, M.M. "Off the Track: Why and How Successful Executives
    Get Derailed", June 2003

viii Maxwell, John, *Developing the Leaders Around You.* Thomas Nelson Publisher, 1995.

ix "The Strategic Leadership Analysis Program", Management Research Group, Portland,
     Maine.

x Welch, Jack, "Putting People First and Strategy Second", *Fortune Magazine* June, 1999.

xi Higgins, Forster. Study of 164 CEOs on Communication, 2006.

xii Larkin, Sandra. *Communicating Change,* University Press, 2002

Printed in the United States
by Baker & Taylor Publisher Services